2

LOST EXETER

LOST EXETER

FIVE CENTURIES OF CHANGE

TODD GRAY

THE MINT PRESS

First published in Great Britain by The Mint Press, 2002
Reprinted 2003

© Todd Gray 2002

Hardback edition ISBN 1-903356-23-7
Softback edition ISBN 1-903356-24-5

Cataloguing in Publication Data
CIP record for this title is available from the British Library

The Mint Press
18 The Mint
Exeter, Devon
England EX4 3BL

Typeset in Frutiger by Kestrel Data, Exeter
Cover design by Delphine Jones

Printed and bound in Great Britain
by Short Run Press Ltd, Exeter

Contents

For Mr Stephen Smith

Foreword

For some two thousand years Exeter has grown and developed, expanding in fits and starts, but ever changing. Its heart remains within the confines of its ancient walls, looking to the river below and out to the surrounding green fields. Many of the changes have been for the better and we have many beautiful buildings that are the legacy from previous generations; other changes have been disastrous – the bombing in 1942 was the single worst event the city has experienced and its effects can still be seen sixty years later. Yet Exeter has continued to prosper because it has adapted to the changing needs of modern life whether lived in the Elizabethan, Georgian or Victorian periods. Those of us who live here are continually reminded of the importance of the ancient environment as we daily pass through the city and yet we need to understand the context of our old buildings – this book firmly sets out that long history of change and development. Local history has never been more popular and I am sure many Exonians will cherish this book as they seek to explore and understand their city further.

Having read and enjoyed this delightful book, I very much recommend it to you all.

The Right Worshipful the Lord Mayor of Exeter
Councillor Val Dixon

Introduction

A common cry heard in modern Exeter is that little is left of the ancient city, that its historic character was ruined by Nazi bombs in 1942 and then by local government officials in the following years. There is a great deal of truth in this: the destruction of one quarter of Exeter in the second world war included a great number of distinguished and much-cherished buildings and many others were lost in the 1950s, 1960s and 1970s through urban schemes.

However, this view demeans the great number of ancient buildings still standing: while it is appalling that so much was lost, it is also possible to be appreciative of the buildings which have survived. But more to the point, this notion of modern Exeter romanticises the past by defining the last sixty years as having been uniquely capable of transforming Exeter and it implies that previous generations were more sympathetic in their treatment of the townscape. Neither are true: astonishing changes took place in other periods and those who lived through them also committed acts of incredible severity which altered Exeter's character. This belief also indicates a fundamental lack of understanding of the general influences, as well as those that were particularly local, which have shaped the townscape. Most of all, it has worrying implications for our ability to save our architectural heritage and to pursue successful future development.

The changes of the last sixty years may feel overwhelming to those who have lived through them but similar comments were made by previous generations and it is simplistic to focus on the twentieth century as the only period of great change, for example the city altered very dramatically in the early 1830s and it also expanded on an extraordinary scale through the long Victorian period.

Change is also responsible for the city we have today in its creation of the positive elements as well as those considered regrettable. Exeter, like all cities, has had a continual process of redevelopment in which demolition or destruction is a necessary part; for two thousand years buildings have been built and subsequently, for the most part deliberately, either renovated, rebuilt or demolished. The city's great wealth in the sixteenth and seventeenth centuries was the means of embellishing the townscape with rich examples of vernacular architecture. By 1942 there had been three centuries of peace with no wartime devastation and until then Exeter had not suffered the great sweeping fires that destroyed other local urban centres such as Tiverton and Honiton. This may have been due many buildings having stone party walls or the lack of thatch in the old walled city from the Elizabethan period if not earlier; the closest thatched building was in Sidwell Street and even that was removed as long ago as 1882.[1] Larger fires happened immediately outside the walls such as in Paris Street in 1717 when some thirty houses were destroyed.[2] Change has instead generally taken place on a piecemeal basis through either accidental fire or deliberate change. Also, no building remains as originally built. The gatehouse to Rougemont Castle has a claim to being the city's oldest building but stands as a ruin and the city walls, although Roman in origin with some sections remarkably intact, is more of a structure and not a building. Instead St Nicholas' Priory and the cathedral are the two oldest surviving complete buildings but neither is true to its Norman origins nor are any others built in the later medieval, Elizabethan, Georgian or Victorian periods. Like all urban centres, Exeter's landscape has had to change and adapt in order to continue to be relevant to modern needs so that it can prosper. Each of the city's best known buildings were built on the site of earlier buildings, for instance the Royal Clarence replaced in part a medieval canon's house,[3] the Royal Albert Memorial Museum stands on the foundations of a row of ancient buildings,[4] and the cathedral was built partly on the site of the Saxon Minster. Arguments could easily be made for the preservation of these older buildings.

What is significantly different about the modern period is the nature of the impetus for change. First of all, it was sudden and secondly, there was an extraordinary scale of damage: a single night's bombing in 1942 transformed the city in an intensity of destruction not seen at least since the Vikings sacked the city one thousand years ago but the details of that attack are so sketchy that it may not have been as devastating as that by the Nazis. Previous change has largely been made on a piecemeal basis. The exceptions have been the 1640s and 1830s. Whereas previous generations in the last one hundred and fifty years or more had been concerned with improving the city, the city council in 1942 had to rebuild. The resulting scale of urban planning was even greater than that undertaken in the 1830s. Since then there has been a perceived failure of these schemes with the general opinion that modern architecture and planning schemes are not of a sufficient standard to match the demolished buildings and a suspicion that all future development will be inadequate. It does not have to be and hopefully more distinctive buildings will some day replace the least appealing post-war ones.

The Cathedral Close is a good example of Exeter's long period of evolution. This is arguably the city's most popular open space but few who relax there on a sunny summer day are likely to know they are resting on a disused graveyard, only feet above the ruins of a Roman garrison town. It is most likely that nearly all visitors, and many residents as well, assume that its airy and open character is ancient and that it has changed little. But, as discussed in more detail below, until relatively recently the Close was closed off by great medieval gates and crowded by some twenty additional buildings which took up possibly as much as a third of the open space enjoyed today. For more than two hundred years there has been a process of 'improvement', of clearing medieval and later buildings to create the open area enjoyed and appreciated by thousands every summer day. Moreover, the buildings around the Close are a blend of styles that largely enhance, and not detract, from its enjoyment.

In order to respond to modern changes it is necessary to understand how the city has changed and appreciate those factors that influenced those changes. It is much easier to tell this story over the last five hundred years than in the medieval period. Even so this history is complex and even with Exeter's unrivalled collection of civic documents it is not possible to give a full account of all of its buildings. Nevertheless much can be learned and this book is concerned with exploring through largely unknown historic images how buildings have changed in the Close and seven other key parts of the townscape being Exe bridges, the *Quartre Voies*, the four ways otherwise known as the Carfax (the junction of High, Fore, South and North Streets), South Street, Goldsmith Street, Queen Street, Bedford Street and Eastgate. These have been chosen for their importance to the city but also because of the richness of the illustrative material. It would be interesting to have included both the quay area and Rougemont Castle but artists appear to have had little interest in them. It may be because the buildings around the river were not of sufficient status or lacked picturesque features. Equally, the demolition of the castle buildings attracted little attention and it may have been that by the early nineteenth century there was little to occupy an artist's attention other than the gatehouse.

EXETER

In comparison to its regional counterparts Exeter has always been the more significant urban centre eclipsing Bodmin, Dorchester, Launceston, and Taunton in terms of size or economic importance. Until the eighteenth century it was more substantial than either Plymouth or Bristol. As the ecclesiastical centre of Devon and Cornwall, the county capital and the commercial hub of a large regional hinterland it was the regional capital. Bristol only recently has been the closest rival city. Exeter was one of the country's largest cities from the fifteenth to late seventeenth centuries but in the early eighteenth century it, along with the rest of the South West, lost ground nationally as other parts of the country industrialised. The result was a small compact city still largely contained within less than 100 acres as defined by the Romans within their mile and a half of ancient walls. The city has had its oval shape cut into four sections by Fore, High, South and North Streets since Roman times, with the street layout remodelled by King Alfred and the four main gates named after compass points.[5] The central point in Exeter throughout this period was the Carfax, the point where the four main streets met and where the Great Conduit was situated.

Exeter has little in common architecturally with its regional rivals and looks surprisingly unlike Plymouth, and even less so Bristol, but is instead similar to many Devon towns. This is partly due to the greater growth of both places in the eighteenth and nineteenth centuries that fundamentally changed their character. Even in respect to church buildings, Plymouth has historically had only one large church while for centuries Exeter has been known for the several dozen small parish churches scattered around the city. The cathedral was the only grand building until the early nineteenth century when Higher and Local Markets were built, but they were not as magnificent as the large public buildings being constructed in much of the rest of the country although for the size of Exeter they were still impressive. Some grand private buildings were being built in the parish of St Leonard's or Pennsylvania but Pennsylvania Park or Bedford Circus, as impressive as they are, were never rivals to the celebrated terraces of Bath or Bristol. At Plymouth the buildings constructed to serve the navy dwarfed any industrial site in Exeter and Dock, later known as Devonport, had far more fashionable houses than Exeter in the early nineteenth century.

Exeter is also less obviously distinctive in its building materials than either Bath or Bristol and closer in appearance to Totnes or Dartmouth. In spite of the Normans defining the city's castle by its red stone, the *rouge mont*, the majority of Exeter's buildings were not faced with it. St Nicholas' Priory is unusual in this respect and even the cathedral hides its volcanic stone behind the veneer of limestone from Salcombe Regis. The city's parish churches were the main 'red' features of the townscape. By the late fifteenth century the tall townhouses of the merchant class, which covered the city particularly in the High Street and in the West Quarter, were nearly always timber fronted with stone sidewalls. Brick, which was being made in East Devon at the end of the sixteenth century, did not become popular in the city until much later. Stone was unusual and it was reserved for some prestigious or institutional buildings, such as most of the clergy houses in the Close, Bampfylde House and Cowick Barton.[6] Wood may have been preferred as it could be highly ornamental and possibly the fashion for glass made it an easier medium to work with. It would be easy to think that the great townhouses of the merchant class were the only residential buildings in the city but their status and solid construction helped them to survive. In comparison, there are no surviving examples of the hovels that the working class lived in. The very nature of these buildings, comprising the largest number in the city, made it unlikely that they would be saved or renovated. Little is known of them but presumably the majority were one-roomed and made of cob or possibly timber-framed.[7]

Exeter's townhouses may have disguised their stone behind their facades but they were not dull. Rather, they were distinctive in the elaborate nature of their fronts which were embellished with carved woodwork, notably animals, mythological beasts and grotesque heads, or elaborate hung slating such as at the Tudor House. Wood allowed rich details whereas the local stone was not suited to carving. The amount of significant carved woodwork in King John's Tavern, the Bear Inn and the Swan Inn could indicate a particular craftsman was at work in the late fifteenth century. The statue of St Peter that stood at the corner of North and High Streets may also be part of his work. The practice of building houses in pairs gave a greater scope to these elaborate designs. All of which was made more impressive given that buildings projected out into the streets, increasing in size with each storey, with large oriel windows impacting onto the townscape.[8]

Until the inter-war years Exeter was dominated by locally-owned shops some of which operated for well over a hundred years. Marks and Spencer (then the Penny Bazaar) opened in 1912 in Queen Street followed by F. W. Woolworth a dozen years later but the majority of retail business was conducted in shops owned and run by local people.[9] There was a long tradition, through to the early nineteenth century, in local merchants having a shop in the ground floor of their townhouses whether on the High Street or elsewhere, a mix of business and residential use. Only later, with the advent of cholera in 1832, did rich merchants begin to move out of the city and maintain a main residence separate from their business. Less wealthy merchants remained in the city, living above their shops. Exeter's nature, in its size and character, makes its history of development much easier to understand.

CHANGE, PROGRESS AND IMPROVEMENT

Like any other expanding city, Exeter has had a continuous process of change with many significant buildings created because of a perceived need to modernise. For example, in the eighteenth century the new law courts and the Devon and Exeter Hospital (now Dean Clarke House) were seen as important embellishments to the built environment. These were just two milestones of change in the last three centuries

which have changed the city's topography: others include the demolition of North Gate in 1769 (followed by the East Gate, the West and Water Gates and the South Gate over the next fifty years), the Great Conduit being demolished in about 1772, the construction of Bedford Circus beginning a year later, a new bridge built over the river at the same time with direct access into the city made by creating New Bridge Street, Southernhay being built in the 1790s, the Exeter Dispensary opening in 1817, the public baths opening four years later, Queen Street being carved out in the 1830s, the railway arriving in 1844 and the running of the first tram at the start of the twentieth century.

Each had a material effect on the life of the city and were no doubt presented as improvements at the time in that they enhanced public life. However, as Hoskins noted in 1960, 'I have been critical of much that is done now in the name of progress whatever that vague word may mean'.[10] Attitudes have differed as to whether each changed the city in a positive or detrimental way: one generation's notions of constructive change are often refuted later. In 1821 the Reverend George Oliver thought that previous generations would regard the notion of civic improvement as a folly because he considered their only motivation had been the making of money. He considered the county and city prison buildings to be a disgrace and 'heartily rejoiced' when Southgate was pulled down. Moreover, he wrote 'During more than half a century the writer has witnessed with inconceivable delight the progressive alterations effected by the Boards of Commissioners of Improvements, Trustees of the Turnpikes, and Directors of the Water Company, to whom Exeter owes a heavy debt of obligation. Rejoicing in the welfare and advancing prosperity of the city, the writer can say with admiration and gratitude, that vast as its physical improvement has been, its moral revolution in the expansion of liberal and Christian feeling has been still greater; and that no reasonable being need seek elsewhere a residence more salubrious, comfortable, polite and friendly'.[11] In 1886 it was T. Northy's opinion that Exeter was 'a city vastly improved, but still improving'.[12]

Hopefully today many people would deplore the demolition of the South Gate and seek to preserve it. In 1890 Edward A. Freeman, the then Oxford Regius Professor of Modern History, noted the passing of the South Gate and recognised the early nineteenth-century need for a new gaol but expressed a wish that the building could have been saved.[13] He also speculated that the demolition of the Treasurer's House in Cathedral Close was 'lamented by the antiquary' but this seems at odds with the evidence. But there were no apparent disagreements at the time and those who saw both

buildings destroyed seemed to agree that they were disgraceful to modern society. In contrast, a generation after Freeman, in 1931, Harbottle Reed, a local architect, wrote 'in an old city like Exeter, ancient buildings, unfortunately, frequently become the victims of vandalism or circumstances and one by one disappear or are modernised out of recognition'.[14] This was the opinion of W. G. Hoskins in 1960 who wrote of Exeter 'Its two greatest enemies are the motor car and the speculative builder . . . The narrow streets are being torn apart and much of old Exeter is being lost because everything must be sacrificed to enable the motorist to go one mile an hour faster or to save his withered legs from a moment's walking . . . In twenty years time, the

1. Sketch of how Exeter's first bridge was imagined in 1904.

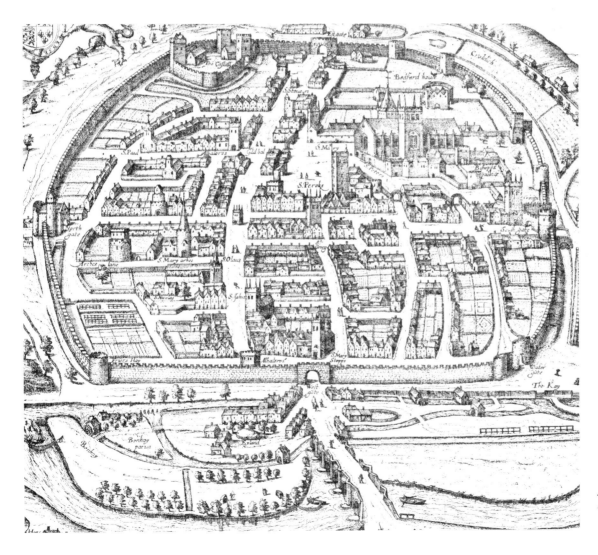

2. Detail of Brawn & Hoghenbegh's map of the city, 1618.

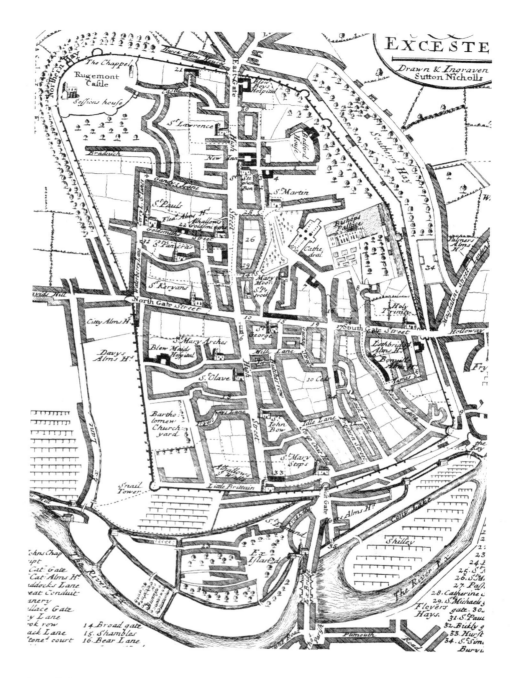

3. Detail of Sutton Nicholl's map of Exeter, 1723, showing the medieval bridge, conduit and gates.

opulent and seemly houses that were built in an age of elegance will have been replaced by a desert of brick and concrete'.[15]

There was not however a time in which society suddenly became concerned with preserving ancient buildings. A public awareness of old buildings is shown in a list of notable Exeter events for the year 1880 published in *The Exeter Flying Post* but even so the paper was noncommittal in merely noting, and not disapproving, of the demolition of the Grammar School and a row of ancient almshouses.[16] In each generation there can be found those who argue for and against the preservation of ancient buildings and artefacts. For example, in the 1820s some voices were raised to preserve Broadgate but the argument of public safety won over aesthetics. In 1823 Henry Ellis noted in his journal:

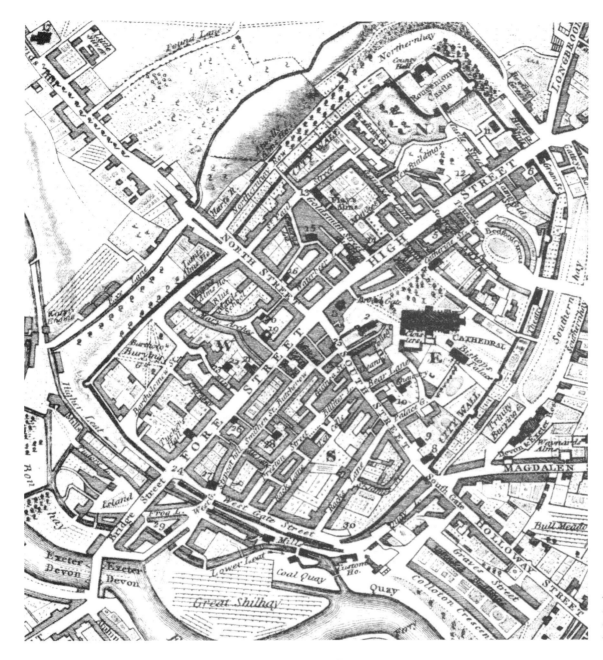

4. Detail of J. Hayman's map of Exeter, 1805, which shows the city before the creation of Queen Street.

This gate the Commissioners of Improvement, in the month of November last, determined on taking down. It was allowed by all persons to be an exceedingly dangerous thoroughfare, but a great fondness being cherished for it by some of the church dignitaries and a few gentlemen antiquarians, they did everything in their power to prevent its demolition. Finding the public voice much against its remaining it was then proposed to re-erect it, so as to form one of the entrances to Northernhay but this suggestion failed.[17]

An adjoining house was pulled down as the first stage but the Dean and Chapter obtained an injunction. Letters were sent to the press expressing objections against the 'modern Goths and Vandals' who were attempting 'with

5. Detail of R. Brown's map of the city, 1835, showing new markets being built, streets more open to traffic and the completion of Bedford Circus.

ruthless and barbarian hands to despoil such a structure'. The counter argument was that the structure was dangerous due to the increase in coaches passing to the Clarence Hotel. One wag suggested that to better please visitors it was appropriate to whitewash the West Front of the cathedral ('so as to please the eye of passengers up and down the Fore Street') while another thought it better to whiten the whole of the North Tower ('imagine the view from Heavitree' as well as the resulting contrast

with the South Tower).[18] The *Exeter Flying Post* printed verses on the destruction of the gate:

> *Broadgate now yields to Gothic sway,*
> *Despoiled of every feature;*
> *St Michael's driven thus away,*
> *The Lord defend St Peter.*[19]

A statue of St Michael was in one of the gate's niches.

6. The model of
eighteenth-century Exeter as built
by Caleb Hedgeland.

Another early proponent of saving buildings was one unidentified Victorian writer who posed as an Exeter schoolboy. He lampooned the taking down of the city's gates by claiming that it was all due to the transport business owned by Robert Russell of South Street. He wrote 'All the historic gates of Exeter were destroyed because they interfered with trade. Mr Russell's wagon was passing through East Gate when a chest of tea came in contact with the arch and much tea was lost. So the tea dealer or wagoner said that our trade was damaged and civilization arrested in consequence of the gate, and it was taken down. And then it was found that the other gates interfered with trade, and they were all one after another destroyed. They might have made a good road on each side, and left the poor gates standing after being there for so many hundreds of years.'[20]

Fashion also plays its part in determining the fate of buildings. In the 1830s, when a great number of fifteenth and sixteenth-century buildings were being demolished in Exeter, it was common for local newspapers to report enthusiastically over the finding of Roman coins but not to comment on the demolished buildings themselves.[21] The Roman period may have been in vogue at the time but decrepit Elizabethan buildings, overcrowded with members of the working class and associated with harbouring disease, were not then fashionable. When the houses were being built, or still nearly new, the city was praised for its High Street: it was as late as 1724 that William Stukeley wrote the 'houses are of a very old but good model, spacious, commodious and not inelegant'. However, tastes quickly changed to a vogue for classical architecture: a generation later, in 1760, Caroline Girle, a visitor from London, thought 'the houses, every one of which are shops, [are] of a most ancient model, indeed we saw not any that can be called good'. Only later, once the city was sanitised and free from the threat of disease, did visitors comment favourably on the city's Elizabethan buildings in viewing them as picturesque.[22]

A striking contrast in opinions can also be seen over the merits of Bedford Circus. In 1911 A. M. Shorto wrote in *The Story of Exeter* that 'We cannot feel that Bedford Circus in any way makes up for the loss of the old [medieval] house'.[23] However, it has been remembered with hindsight as Exeter's best example of Georgian architecture.[24] Moreover, Edward Freeman thought only 21 years before Shorto that the importance of the circus was that it symbolised a sea change in the city's population: in his view it exhibited 'features of a watering place' and attracted a group, that is retired gentry and professional people from other parts of the country, that had not hitherto resided in Exeter.[25]

These personal opinions reflect wider senses of taste and fashion from the times in which they were expressed. In 1862 one speaker at a meeting of the Exeter Diocesan Architectural Society noted that on High Street there could be seen, and enjoyed, a diverse range of Elizabethan, Georgian and Victorian Gothic townhouses. But he expressed the view that the 'tall, thin, flat-faced, flat-topped style' of Exeter's High Street buildings was uncouth and thought more favourably of the traditional 'lofty gables, sharp-angled dormers and corbelled oriels'.[26]

The desire for different styles of architecture can often be based on financial rather than aesthetic grounds. In about 1931 an American visitor was told of the unsuccessful attempts to demolish one of the city's oldest merchant houses in Fore Street. Charles Brooks wrote:

I was told this tavern anecdote in Rougemont Castle by a man in a shabby coat and with the listless bearing that goes with want of work. Plainly he was disgusted with Exeter's lack of progress. He had once been in New York City. He was afire with enthusiasm for tall buildings, and already in his fancy he saw Exeter's skyline pierced by lofty towers of commerce.[27]

His vision of an Exeter like that of Manhattan, of a landscape filled with Debenham Towers, is impossible to imagine.

7. The Higher Market, as drawn by Dennis Flanders in 1938. It escaped the threatened destruction of Thomas Mawson's redevelopment of Exeter in 1911 but was only partially retained in the redevelopment of the city following war damage in 1942.

PERCEPTIONS OF CHANGE

Over the last two centuries Exeter residents have expressed opinions that they personally witnessed overwhelming changes in the city's topography. For instance Henry Ellis, a jeweller who lived adjacent to the Turk's Head, wrote in 1833 that 'the alterations and improvements which have taken place in our good city even within my recollection have most materially altered the character of the place'.[28] Philip Chilwell De La Garde wrote in 1862 that the shops of the High Street had 'so changed their character, within my recollection, as hardly to be recognised. The vast sheets of plate-glass, the sumptuous frames of brass and bronze in which they are set, and the costly goods arrayed behind them would, forty years ago, have been deemed incredible.'[29] In 1876 James Garrey Cossins, a former tobacconist then aged 63 years who lived in a Mount Dinham cottage, wrote 'persons who have been absent from Semper Fidelis for many years, on re-visiting the old city, declare that it is improved and so much altered that they cannot recognise some of the localities'.[30] Just a few years after the second world war Professor W. G. Hoskins wrote 'Before the Germans wrecked it, Exeter was one of the most beautiful and appealing cities in England, full of colour, light and movement'.[31] That its citizens have felt Exeter has altered beyond recognition in their lifetimes is almost always attributable to the city's history that, for at least the last five centuries, has been one of continual change.

A number of Exeter men recorded individual changes in their journals. Thomas Granger of Rougemont House continually made such entries: he noted Palace Gate being taken down in 1812, the new church of St Sidwell opening in 1813, the demolition of both Bear and West Gates and the widening of Palace Gate (street) in 1814 and 1815, the foundation stone of St David's church being laid in 1816 and that of the new city prison in 1818, the loss of St Martin's Gate in 1820 and of St Catherine's Gate two years later. He also noted the new

spire on St Sidwell's church in 1823, Broadgate being taken down from 1824 to 1825, the completion of Bedford Circus in 1825, the new sewers being laid in 1833, attempts to level Fore Street and improve Bridge Street in 1834 as well as several openings being made from Fore Street into Butchers' Row in 1833 and 1834, and the opening of the two new markets in 1836 and 1838.[32] William Nation, a local banker, also made similar notes in his journal. In August 1811 he recorded:

During the last few months the [cathedral's] churchyard underwent great alterations & improvements. One half the avenue of Trees leading from Broadgate to the west door of the Cathedral was felled & many feet of the yard on the Northern side was taken in, in order to make a spacious road. The road from the western end of the Church to Martin's gate was destroyed & gravelled like the other parts of the Yard. Palace gate was taken down & the road from thence to the Canonry at the Cloister gate was very considerably widened.

And in 1825 he wrote:

In the first week of this month commenced the demolition of Broadgate which led from the High Street into the Close opposite the West end of the Cathedral: the last of the gates of the Close, & indeed the last of the ancient gates of the City.[33]

Topographical change has fascinated the people of Exeter for hundreds of years. The pulling down of buildings has often been a spectator sport. In 1833, when houses were being demolished around Broadgate, a small crowd gathered to watch. A local shop owner recorded the event:

when from want of sufficient care, a considerable portion of one of them fell with a terrific crash, raising a dense cloud of dust which came in great force into the High Street, and with it came helter-skelter – a number of

8. Pencil sketch by George Townsend of the 'Night Men' who were responsible for the sanitation of the streets, mid nineteenth century.

9. The panelled room from 229 High Street that was sold to the Nelson-Atkins Museum, Kansas, in the 1930s.

persons, principally idlers, who had been watching the operations, and pretty figures many of them presented, rubbing dust out of their eyes, with which they were covered from head to foot! Fortunately however, no lives were lost.[34]

Finally, improvement, or merely change, could be welcomed in theory but not in practice. When in 1854 Reverend George Oliver heard about plans to remove the archway between the buildings of St Nicholas' Priory he objected on the grounds that he had, at the age of 74 and having lived in those rooms for 47 years, been promised that he would be able to reside there in 'undisturbed possession' for the term of his life. Improvement, he thought, should begin at the opposite end of The Mint, and only with the permission of the owner.[35]

PERIODS OF CHANGE

Exeter has had seven[36] periods of short intensive topographical change; these were the 1530s, 1642 to 1646, 1769 to 1784, the 1830s, the 1930s, 1942 and the late twentieth century. The character of each was particularly different.

In the 1530s the Reformation resulted in a certain amount of alterations to Exeter's buildings. The Priory of St Nicholas was privatised and became home to one of the city's Protestant merchants[37] in the same way as Buckland Abbey was the home of Sir Richard Grenville and later of Sir Francis Drake. Polsloe Priory, the Franciscan Friary outside the South Gate and the Dominican Friary, where Bedford Circus later stood and where Bedford Street is now, were all closed and their property placed in private ownership. The church, cloister and chapter house at St Nicholas' Priory were demolished as were buildings at Polsloe Priory and several other religious houses in and around the city.

Nearly a century later there was another short episode of change when many of the buildings outside the city walls were destroyed during the two sieges of Exeter: when John Taylor, the king's Water Poet, visited in 1649 he found 'this mad fire of contention turned all to ruins, rubbage, cinders, ash and fume'.[38] After the war Exeter people looked out onto the eastern suburb of Sidwell that lay in ruins. Houses in four parishes, St Sidwell, St Thomas, St David and St Edmund, were greatly destroyed in 1645. It was claimed that as many as 80 houses were demolished in the suburbs. It is thought that every house from the East Gate to St Anne's Chapel, all those between Exe Bridge and the hospital, and many of those outside the South Gate in the parish of Trinity were utterly destroyed.[39] Much of Exeter outside the walls lay in ruins.

These were two brief periods of change driven by national events and to some extent experienced by much of England. However, two greater phases of change were in the late eighteenth century and in the late 1820s and 1830s that were driven by forces within the city itself. It was the opinion of Edward Ashworth, the Victorian architect, that the years 1768 to 1779 were a 'terrible time for public improvements in Exeter' and he noted as casualties the North Gate, the Great Conduit, the Exe Bridge, Bedford House, the church of Allhallows on the Walls and the ancient building which the Clarence Hotel replaced.[40] Curiously he overlooked the East Gate, one of the great symbols of Exeter, which was demolished only a few years later. Each of these, with the exception of Bedford House and the Cathedral Close building, was pulled down to enhance the flow of traffic. At this time Exeter was mostly within its ancient walls but straining at the seams. Some public buildings had already been erected outside, notably the Workhouse built on Heavitree Road in the late 1690s and the Devon and Exeter Hospital in Southernhay in 1743. Large numbers of people lived in the parishes immediately outside the city, notably St Sidwell and St Thomas, but the ancient city was still the centre.

Traffic congestion was responsible for the changes.

10. Photograph of the New Inn, 25-6 High Street, 1913, which was destroyed in the bombing of 1942. It was probably a mid fifteenth-century building erected by the Dean and Chapter a few buildings to the north of St Stephen's church. The building began as an inn but became known as the Merchants, or Common, Hall because it became the base for the city's cloth trade. The city leased the building and required that cloth purchased by 'foreign' merchants had to pass through the hall; in 1601 twelve London men involved in the cloth trade rented rooms, or parts of them, during three cloth fairs.[42] The building was rebuilt in about 1688 and ceased to be an inn in the 1770s. Its great architectural feature was the Apollo Room, a 32½ foot long room with an ornate plaster ceiling by Thomas Lane who depicted the Royal Arms and those of the See and City of Exeter. In 1779 there was bull baiting in the street outside the building to celebrate the 5th of November.[43] The inn was probably at its most popular in the early to mid eighteenth century. By 1849 it was the premises of Messrs. Green and Bennett (later Green and Son), drapers, and by 1913 the Apollo Room was used as a 'Mantle and Fur Showroom'. From 1923 to 1942 it was owned by Bobby & Company.

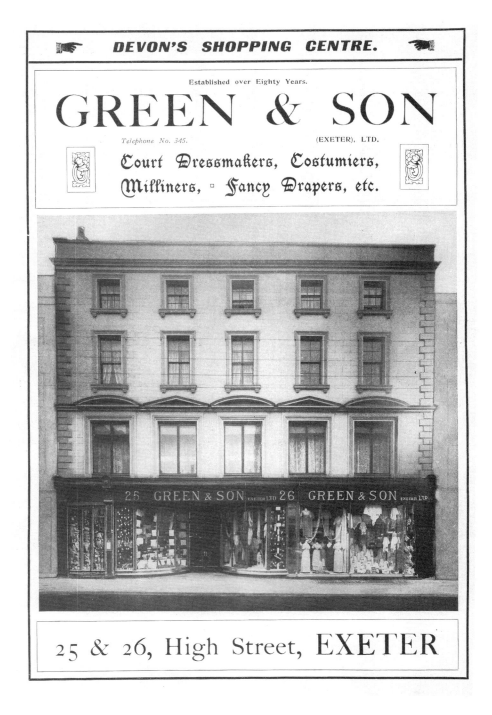

DEVON'S SHOPPING CENTRE.

Established over Eighty Years.

GREEN & SON

Telephone No. 345.   (EXETER), LTD.

Court Dressmakers, Costumiers, Milliners, ▫ Fancy Drapers, etc.

25 & 26, High Street, EXETER

There were only two ways of crossing the city, one was via South and North Streets and the other was down High Street and Fore Street but Exe Bridge was reached only by turning off at West Street to the bottom of Stepcote Hill through the West Gate. Moreover, Exeter did not have indoor markets; goods, notably foodstuffs, were purchased in the open streets and stalls filled up what little space there was. Streets were so narrow that it was later claimed that a man could reach out from the windows of his upper floor windows and nearly the shake the hand of his neighbour.[41] Although Exeter may appear to have been extraordinarily restricted in early twentieth century terms, the scale of it was far greater in 1800. A cursory glance at Hedgeland's model of eighteenth-century Exeter shows the extent of the crowding. As impossible as it is to comprehend by modern standards, Parliament Street was a useful, and not totally unusual, thoroughfare. In the 1770s a new Exe Bridge was built so that it was possible to travel directly into Fore Street. The Great Conduit, which stood at the crossways of Fore, High, South and North Streets, was removed to allow the free passage of pedestrians, horses and carts, and the East and North Gates were taken down to open up access into the city. Although Exeter was no longer at the edge of modern technology, its own industrial revolution having taken place in the late sixteenth and early seventeenth centuries, it was still a prosperous and growing city. The increase in population and traffic meant that the medieval street layout was confined and congested. When the Great Conduit was about to be demolished an unknown writer, who used the nom-de-plume of Civis, gleefully wrote in the *Exeter Flying Post* that 'no longer will the water spouts annoy us'.[44]

The years that followed this Georgian burst of civic change, the first few decades of the nineteenth century, were more notable for the buildings going up rather than those being taken down. Private money was speculated on creating Colleton Crescent, Pennsylvania Park, Southernhay and Baring Crescent, just some of the fine buildings erected on largely green field sites. Expansion also took place within the city: Bedford Circus began in the 1770s and became a reality some twenty years later. City officials did continue to demolish public buildings, such as the West and Water Gates in 1815, which changes were in the character of those of a generation before. There were two other striking demolitions. The first was the pulling down in 1819 of the South Gate, which housed the city's prison, and it took Holy Trinity Church with it. Condemned for its unsuitability, this ancient building was replaced by a new prison erected on the site of the current Rougemont Hotel. The second was the removal of the Broadgate in the 1820s. It was the last surviving medieval gate. In the first three decades of the nineteenth century the character of rapid building and much slower demolition continued apparently with public approval and without much dissent.

The arguments may have been reserved for the very-heated discussions over controversial plans to remove Exeter's markets from the open air to a purpose-built market. In 1818 the Chamber felt that the city had outgrown the existing markets in regards to convenience and sanitation. Three years later George Oliver noted in his history of Exeter that it gave 'an opportunity of clearing away the encumbrances of several blind alleys and crowded courts, and of introducing perfect ventilation and cleanliness, whilst the health and comfort of the buyers and sellers were attended to'.[45] In 1827 Henry Ellis had complained that the pork market diminished his profits as a jeweller in the High Street and wrote that the pannier market was less objectionable because it was not unsightly and the traders left at a reasonable hour. However, Ellis was scathing about uncouth butchers who blocked the High Street all day with their stalls. That year he wrote:

I remember on one occasion a highly respectable gentleman from the country stopping at my door in his phaeton and being bawled at by one of the queasy rascals to 'move on!' as he wanted to bring up his cart with some pork. The gentleman, who was a little deaf, not hearing him or if he did not choosing to obey such an imperative command, remained stationary, when the brute bellowed again at the very top of his voice 'I say! Get out of the way you blue-coated son of a—.[46]

Arguments were heard over where the market should be cited with local opinions shaped over concerns on the effect on property values, lost trade, building costs, and allegations of corruption and self-interest within local government.[47] It took another fifteen years, until the year 1833, before the city agreed but instead of one building it was decided there would be two. Lower, or Western, Market was carved out of the area between Fore and Smythen Streets, taking with it a portion of Butchers' Row. The market opened in 1835. Higher, or Eastern, Market was created by demolishing the existing fish, potato and oat markets at the northern end of Goldsmith Street. A temporary market for pork opened between Gandy and Goldsmith Streets in the area that later became Higher Market[48] and the second new market opened in 1838. But it is telling that this, the fiercest of Exeter's disputes, was about the erection of a building and not about the demolition of one. No evidence has been found of complaints in demolishing any of the fifteenth and sixteenth-century buildings in Butchers' Row to make way for Lower Market.

When in 1833 public agreement was finally reached there was a new urgency for change. The years from 1769 to 1831 were more moderate in their changes than those in the following decade. The overriding factor was the cholera epidemic that gripped the city in the summer of 1832. Infectious disease may not have been the cause for Exeter's Improvement Act of 1833 but it was the driving force for implementation.

Cholera had been a worry to the city's inhabitants for some time before it arrived that summer but the danger had occasionally been taken lightly: in the previous December it was reported that a couple living in Frog Lane suspected they had the disease. In the middle of the night the husband sought to stave it off by giving his wife brandy, generally thought of as a preventative. He later woke to more complaints and passed her the bottle but found his wife hours later with ink-black bowels and sent for the doctor who pronounced her condition without hope. After hours of discomfort a neighbour discovered the error: the husband exclaimed 'Christ Jesus! This is all my doing and if I hadn't passed the

bottle of ink from the shelf instead of the brandy bottle'.[49]

It was no longer possible for newspapers to make light about the threat of disease in the summer of 1832 when hundreds of Exeter people died. There was an added irony in early September when John Nicholls of New Bridge Street died of cholera: he was an Improvement Commissioner.[50] His death would have been yet another reminder of the seriousness of improving the city. Exeter, like the rest of the country, was politically torn by the calls for reform of both national and local government. A report from the national government into Exeter concluded that the local politicians were 'self-elected and conducting their affairs in private' with the result that they 'have not gained the confidence of the inhabitants'. One issue was the membership of the Improvement Commission amid widespread concerns over undue influence of the city's officials.[51] The parliamentary act reformed the Commission and when the newly-elected members met there were an unprecedented number of proposals, 33 in all, for change within the city. These included the creation of three new streets and a footpath to open up the city, removing the South Street Conduit and steps from the Grammar School in High Street, setting back buildings, removing projections from others (presumably overhanging windows or porches) and the entire demolition of a number of buildings.[52]

Over the next few years the Commissioners were responsible for a series of momentous improvements. In 1835 to 1836 a new cut, eventually known as Queen Street, was made from High Street to the new Higher Market. Previously there had only been a passage way marked by two posts on High Street and carts travelled through the lane leading to what is now Gandy Street.[53] Fore, South and North Streets were fundamentally changed with buildings demolished or 'projections' removed such as porches, windows or archways. In 1834 there was considerable work done to the gradient of the hill of Fore Street: the steepness was moderated by raising Lower Bridge Street and the hill itself was dug out[54] by as much as four feet.[55]

The narrowness of South Street in the early 1830s is hard for modern residents of Exeter to conceive. In 1876 one writer impressed upon his readers that 'an idea may be formed of the former width when I say that the upper parts of some of the houses were just within shaking hands distance'.[56] Nearly fifty years earlier, in 1828, a guide to the city noted that projections from the top of South Street to Bear Street had long been the subject of public complaint because they made it too narrow to allow two carriages to pass in the street. It was hoped that this 'evil' would soon be successfully dealt with.[57] Through the 1830s houses were fully or partly demolished to widen the street: King John's Tavern was one of the many buildings that were rebuilt at this time. In 1834 the house at the corner of South and Fore Street was set back which led to 'the alteration or removal and rebuilding of all the houses as far as St George's church'.[58] The church itself was demolished nine years later. In 1833 one Commissioner made the case for widening the passageway to the church of St George based on the particular circumstances of butchers. It was reported he had claimed they were 'a class of persons the comfort and convenience of whom had been much neglected. He said that persons of this class, and their wives too, were generally of pretty portly appearance.' His argument was the size of the passageway made it impossible for these fat butchers and their wives to walk together to church 'as they should'.[59]

It was possible to pull down part of these buildings because of the way in which they were constructed. The roof timbers rested on the stone walls built between each property. Demolition was made easier by the number of buildings built on long strips of land. Thus it was possible to pare off the length of each building and retain part of the property. It would then be refaced in a more modern style.

The entrance to North Street was widened from its original width of some twelve feet by pulling down houses. The steepness of the Longbrook valley was improved by lowering the gradients of the hills on either side and by the erection of the Iron Bridge from 1834 to 1835. New North Road was laid out in 1833 and connected the corner of Sidwell Street with St David's Hill.

These were all improvements designed to meet the needs of an increasing level of traffic. But after the loss of more than 400 lives to cholera in 1832 the Commissioners were also aware of issues of health.[60] The West Quarter was the least savoury part of Victorian and early twentieth-century Exeter; in 1833 Mr W. P. Kingdom, a Commissioner, said that it was 'a sink of impurity, the stronghold of disease and the nurse of crime'.[61] This part of the city, though not the wealthiest, still had some rich merchants but had been reduced to being the poorest part of Exeter. The irony was noted at the time. In 1886 T. J. Northy wrote in his *Popular History of Exeter* that in the West Quarter 'They herded together like swine, grovelled in filth, led profligate lives, and lived in houses, and in situations, which were overcrowded and unhealthy. Many of the dwellings, however, were formerly the residences of opulent citizens; and some of those remaining in our worst neighbourhoods today are interesting as specimens of ancient architecture.'[62] These were the same sentiments of an earlier Exeter resident: in 1824 Henry Ellis wrote of the West Quarter 'in these back lanes were many good houses inhabited formerly by the principal merchants of the place . . . built at the corner of one of these streets one of the best houses in the city; quite a mansion in its day. This house with its spacious rooms richly corniced ceilings, solid mahogany doors and handsome staircase is now the residence of squalid poverty . . . the shock head of the porter, coal heaver or navvy protrudes through the windows of the upper stories into the streets as he smokes his long or short pipe squirting the fragrant fluid on the luckless passengers below!'[63]

11-12. The initial sketch of George Townsend, 1874, with his finished work. See pages 34-5.

13. Undated painting attributed to John Gendall of Numbers 255 to 258 High Street, including the Rose & Crown Inn. On the back was written, possibly by Thomas Shapter, 'Opposite the lower end of Grammar School on right hand looking down from Eastgate by Gendall. The figures sitting down are portraits of an old couple living in Coffin's Court. Miss Tucker was sister to Tucker the artist.' Hannah Tucker was a fruitier at Number 256 High Street, Francis T. Richards, a cooper, was at Number 257 and at Number 255 was A. E. Abraham, optician.[87]

The Commissioners attempted to do their part in stopping the spread of disease by spending one thousand pounds in covering drains and washing the streets.[64] They also attempted to increase ventilation by removing 'obstructions' such as one of the archways in Mint Lane. It took another generation before the archway between the priory buildings was demolished.[65] Although a small city by modern standards, Exeter was a confined and crowded place. When New North Road was completed in 1842 Henry Ellis of the High Street noted that it enabled him 'in a few minutes to breathe the fresh air of the country without the drawback in going and returning a long distance through streets'.[66]

A hundred years later there was yet another spur to change. After the first world war the national government assessed the country's housing stock and embarked on a course to eliminate the city's slums. In 1930 each urban and district council were required to submit five year plans for clearing unfit housing. By this date Exeter had already built more than a thousand homes for the working class and demolished parts of the ancient city such as Paul Street. The city council concentrated their efforts on the West Quarter and pulled down many old buildings that were clearly substandard. The city's 'fairy godmother' was Miss Wills, who had already given Honeylands, the former country house in Whipton that is still used to provide medical care for children. She also provided funds to build flats with modern facilities in the West Quarter. However, there was a great deal of controversy over whether landlords were being adequately compensated when buildings were pulled down and over the way in which properties were demolished and replaced. Some were unhappy about being taken out of their homes and placed outside the city in new estates, notably Burnthouse Lane. One Exeter man compared it to being sent to Siberia. The

14. A detail of the imaginative artistic device that was intended to provide a title and focus for the painting.

rector of St Mary Major wrote that 'slums will never be cured by the mere removal to better surroundings' and predicted that instead of one in the West Quarter there would be five such areas in the city. And one visitor who was lecturing from London admonished his Exeter audience by saying 'Your Cathedral is a disgrace to Christianity when it is compared to the houses around the corner'.[68]

There was also a great deal of controversy over whether it was right to save any of the older buildings in the West Quarter. The sum of £2,000 was estimated to refurbish two buildings on Stepcote Hill but councillors argued over justifying the costs. But one councillor looked back to recent years and claimed that their 'predecessors when they wiped out historical features of the city destroyed that which would have been a gold mine of income for visitors today'.[69] There seemed to be a clear division between those who saw the old Elizabethan buildings for their historic worth and those who viewed them as unsanitary and responsible for harbouring disease. But the programme of slum clearance changed the entire character of the West Quarter and

moved a good part of the residents to the new estates outside the city into the suburbs.

There were other particular forces for change in the 1930s. In 1930 the Church of England decided to demolish several churches in Exeter on the grounds that they were redundant. Four were destroyed (including the churches of St John and St Paul) but two were saved through the campaigning of local people. Unfortunately both of these, Bedford Chapel and the church of St Lawrence, were destroyed twelve years later when the Luftwaffe bombed the city.[70] In that decade a threat to Exeter's buildings came from overseas: French & Company, an American architectural salvage firm, sent agents to the city to find ancient building materials which would be of interest to North American clients. Thousands of pounds were offered for ancient rooms and it was through these endeavours that the panelling of Number 229 High Street was acquired and exported to the United States. It remains there, in a museum in Kansas.[71]

As sweeping as the schemes for slum clearance, among the others, were, the events of 5 May 1942 were much greater in their effects. The fire bombs dropped by the Nazi planes destroyed some 1,500 homes as well as the City Library, the Lower Market, the City Hospital and six churches as well as three quarters of the main shopping area. Nearly a hundred people died.[72] The German attack was not totally unexpected. Only a few weeks previously there had been some bombing in the city. No doubt some residents of Exeter would have remembered events in 1911, only a few years before the first world war, when several German airships passed over Exeter and caused great concern. At that time one resident remembered a similar incident two years previously when locals had also thought they were about to be invaded. In 1911 the airships passed over Stoke Hill towards Thorverton and it was observed that 'no harm came. The hostile airships vanished into air, and we were left scathless'.[73]

However, Exeter was not so lucky a generation later.

15. This is one ancient church that has not survived: of the thirty that existed in the thirteenth century only six are left. St John's church was located on Fore Street and only one wall exists. This was a medieval building and the only other church in the city with a bow in addition to St Stephen. Others were found in The Mint. In the early nineteenth century the main entrance to Butchers' Row was through Fore Street and under the bow but it was later claimed that the entrance was so narrow that some carts had to partially unload their meat. Another entrance was through Milk Street but it was so narrow that in order to turn the corner meat was removed from the stalls in order to give room for a horse's head to pass.[74] In 1806 Jenkins considered that the building was in good repair[75] but from March to May in 1864 the bow was removed on the grounds it was unsafe. There was a great deal of disagreement in the parish regarding pulling it down: in November 1863 Bishop Philpotts had written 'I can see no reason why I should attempt to screen you from any unpleasant consequence which may arise from your non-repair of your parish church . . . it is not to be expected that people will help those who show no disposition to help themselves'. The parish held a vote the following month to decide whether to impose a local rate for funds but 108 parishioners voted for it and 108 against. The rector cast a deciding vote for the rate but the attempts to save the bow failed.[76] In April 1864 a special meeting of the city's Improvement Commissioners wrote to the bishop that the reinstatement of the bow would not be in the public's convenience and be injurious to its morals: they thought that it restricted light and air, obstructed carriages from entering from Fore Street and that the passage of pedestrians under the bow was unseemly during service.[77] The bishop disagreed but the bow was never rebuilt. In 1937 the church was demolished but the tower lasted until 1957 when it was removed as a public nuisance.[78]

The bombing in 1942 was the greatest single act to change the city's topography and history and set a great challenge to local government officials on rebuilding. The Council commissioned Thomas Sharp, a town planner, to prepare a development plan for Exeter. His *Exeter Phoenix: a plan for rebuilding* was printed in 1946 but only part of it was followed. It included the rebuilding of High Street, the creation of a Princesshay and the carving out of Western Way, one of the two inner bypass schemes. Much of the council's efforts were outside of the historic centre, including the creation of industrial parks at Sowton and Marsh Barton and the building of housing estates throughout what had been surrounding villages. It is difficult to summarise the events of these post-war years because little has yet been written. The Council's own view of its role was made in *Exeter's planning achievements*, a booklet published in the 1990s. It was admitted that 'the city has not always treated its heritage well and many historic buildings were lost to the bulldozer' and that the council acted more sympathetically in the years after 1977 because of increasing public awareness.[79]

The House That Moved is a bittersweet symbol of the council's achievements. It was widely lauded for saving this fifteenth-century building from destruction at its site in Frog Street in 1961 but the irony is that a building of similar age and significance was destroyed at the site to which it moved. Other undertakings at this time were also made at considerable, and often questionable, costs. These post-Sharp schemes remain the least popular, and most damning, of the council's achievements.

But Exeter was rebuilt. The eastern end of High Street, constructed in the 1950s, is generally regarded as bland or undistinguished[80] but it is at least functional and follows the street pattern set centuries ago. However, the brutal carving of Western Way out of the city centre necessitated the destruction of many early buildings beneath Westgate and along Magdalen Street, caused as much by official inaction and the resulting blight, and

while no doubt it has improved the flow of traffic it is also disjointed and unappealing. Cars are now parked where families lived for centuries. This road effectively cut the river and quayside from the city centre with one consequence being that there is a continuing dilemma on how to connect what is effectively the city's main recreational area to its commercial heart. It also isolated the medieval Exe bridge within busy traffic and the tower of the church of St Edmund sits like a tombstone on the bridge. The creation of the Guildhall Shopping Centre in the early 1970s was just as insensitive in causing the demolition of important buildings in North Street, the destruction of medieval streets and it transformed Paul Street into what must be the least attractive public way in the city. The most positive description that the definitive guide to the county's buildings has for the Guildhall Shopping Centre is 'mediocre'.[81]

The last thirty years has been more positive with detailed information about sites and buildings channelled from the Exeter Archaeological Unit (created in 1971) that provides the basic framework for understanding the significance of threatened buildings. There have been more sensitive schemes such as those at Carpenter Close on Bartholomew Street East and Shilhay. Even so, the best, or at least the more distinctive, modern architecture lies outside the city centre within the Exeter University campus or in the business/industrial estates.

Debenhams, Renslade House and Exeter College are perhaps the most visible disappointments from these years, a reminder that size is indeed not everything. It is equally difficult to like any modern building along the length of Sidwell Street, a serious rival to Paul Street for the title of Exeter's Ugliest Street. The Exeter Civic Society has produced the only publication on modern architecture in Exeter but it would be difficult to arouse much public enthusiasm for many of the highlighted buildings.[82] Within the centre perhaps only Exeter Library, built in 1965, or the end building in Castle Street, built in 1989,[83] would receive much praise but even the library today looks tired and uninspired. Without doubt these are questions of personal taste and greatly influenced by prevailing fashion. Possibly it is not only the buildings' poor building materials that make them unpopular but also the period in which they were built remains unappreciated. Equally, there has been considerable public debate over the merits of the redevelopment of Princesshay in which opinions have been divided on the value of preserving this post-war shopping precinct.

Only buildings within the city walls, or immediately outside of them, are examined in this study. Many other interesting buildings of greater Exeter have also been destroyed. For instance, Bowhill has not survived. This eighteenth-century mansion was in St Thomas and is often confused with the medieval building also known as Bowhill House. The St Thomas Hospital for Lunatics occupied the building from 1801 to 1869 when it moved to new premises in Wonford. The building was opened in 1801 and extended two years later.[84] In the years up to 1862 it housed 1,746 patients, 889 of whom were discharged and considered cured. Their daily newspapers were *The Telegraph* and *The Times*. The new building at Wonford was begun in 1866 and opened on 7 July 1869 as The Wonford Home for the Insane. Curiously, it doesn't appear as though the patients moved from Bowhill until 6 October.[85] A strike by stonemasons and wallers had previously delayed the building in 1868, possibly extending the time at Bowhill.[86] In 1870 the verandah and clock were removed from Bowhill and placed on the new building at Wonford.[87] Bowhill House was not considered an appropriate building by the 1860s[88] and the building was demolished sometime around 1871.[89] Bricks were used to build homes in Pennsylvania's Edgerton Park.[90] It is beyond the scope of this book to mention the dozens of other notable buildings outside the city walls which merit discussion.

With all the recent developments and those which are on the horizon it is essential to have as full an understanding as possible of the events of the past in order to make informed judgements on how best to respond to inevitable changes to the city's topography. The following eight sections aim to provide an account of how the city has evolved in these key parts of the townscape through changes to individual buildings caused by fire, war and notions of improvement and progress. The majority of the illustrations, mostly sketches, drawings, paintings and photographs with a few prints, are unpublished and come from collections in the Devon & Exeter Institution, Devon Record Office, Exeter Cathedral Archives, Royal Albert Memorial Museum and the Westcountry Studies Library. There are several sequences of illustrations including three copies by Edward Shapter of views by Henry Oxenham, four retrospective drawings of Queen Street by F. Algar in the 1920s, four large detailed paintings by John Gendall of various locations in the city as well as a series of sketches showing South Street being redeveloped in the mid 1830s. Nevertheless, the book is dominated by the work of John Gendall and George Townsend. Gendall lived from 1790 to 1865 and was a distinguished water-colourist who was nevertheless described in 1856 as a 'carver, gilder and print seller'. He lived in High Street and Cathedral Yard. Among his works are the series of views depicting the cholera outbreak in 1832 and *Etched Views of Exeter* (1834). Townsend lived from 1813 to 1894. He styled himself 'artist, lithographer and drawing master' and was based in the High Street but lived in Deanery Place. Among his works were the two series of *Views in Devonshire* (1848-71, 1853-c.75). What makes their work of particular interest is that both men were greatly concerned with old buildings and recorded those that were about to be demolished. They also did retrospective views. The most informative of these drawings, watercolours and initial sketches are included in this book to help explain how Exeter's townscape has developed over the last five hundred years together with the work of more than a dozen artists.

Acknowledgements

I would like to thank John Allan, Stuart Blaylock, Tony Collings, Richard Parker and Professor Malcolm Todd who have generously shared their detailed knowledge of the topographical development of Exeter and John Draisey and Margery Rowe for their advice and assistance on the city's archives, all of whom have saved me from making many terrible mistakes and omissions. I am grateful to Ian Maxted for sharing his expertise on Devons prints. Any and all remaining errors are of course my own. I am very appreciative of the support from Exeter City Council, notably the foreword kindly supplied by the Lord Mayor and of the help given by the staff, in particular I would like to thank Janet Henderson. I am once again in awe of the creativity of Delphine Jones who has provided such an extraordinary cover and grateful to Andy Jones for his production advice. I am also very grateful to the staffs of the Devon & Exeter Institution, Devon Record Office, Exeter Cathedral Archives and Westcountry Studies Library for their patience over many years. Tony Rouse has been, as always, a great source of knowledge on illustrations and printed sources. Permission to publish illustrations has very kindly been given by Devon & Exeter Institution, Devon Record Office, Exeter Cathedral Archives, the Isca Collection, Exeter City Museums and Art Gallery and Westcountry Studies Library. I am also grateful to Professor Joyce Youings for the loan of a photograph of an illustration formerly in the possession of Miss Norah Drew. Finally I would like to thank Land Securities for their grant that has made this book possible.

St Peter stood for some five centuries overlooking the Carfax and was a silent witness to the changes to the city caused by religious turmoil, war, fire, commercial pressure, traffic congestion and civic improvement.

1. Exe Bridges

For the last ten centuries at least six bridges, built in the twelfth, thirteenth, eighteenth and twentieth centuries, have crossed the Exe at, or very near to, the present site of Exe Bridges. Remnants of some of them remain.

1. Willem Schellinks' view was drawn in 1662. Schellinks, a Dutchman, considered the bridge to be 'fine'.[93]

Exe Bridge, drawn in 1772.
Partially demolished in about 1778.

A medieval seventeen-arched stone bridge, built in about 1200, which replaced a timber bridge at what had been a ford across the river Exe, the first crossing from the sea. At one end stood St Thomas' church (destroyed by flooding in the fifteenth century and rebuilt at its present site) and at the other were St Edmund's church and a small chantry chapel.[91] The bridge was made redundant by the building of a new bridge in the late eighteenth century (see Illustration 9) but only partly demolished:

the arches over the river were taken down but the eastern portion of the bridge continued in use as Edmund Street and St Edmund's church was itself in service until 1956. In 1773 one visitor wrote that the bridge, then still standing, was 'incommodious, inelegant and ruinous'.[92] In 1821 George Oliver, who was born a few years after the bridge was dismantled, wrote that this entrance to Exeter had been 'circuitous, confined, precipitous and dangerous'. The building of the replacement bridge took several years, partly because of concerns over the ability of the builder, and in that time flooding carried away the foundation stones and caused concerns for

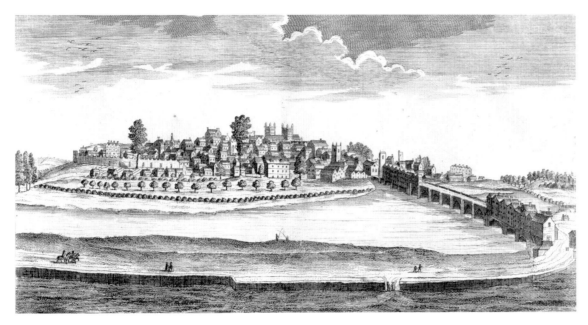

2. William Stukeley's engraving of Exeter represents the bridge to have been more like those at Barnstaple and Bideford that cross a long stretch of low-lying mud and marsh. He noted in 1724 that it was 'of great length, and has houses on both sides and both ends; a considerable void space in the middle; there is a church upon it with a great steeple'.[95]

3. John Eveleigh's drawing of the medieval bridge in 1772 shows houses built on all the spans of the bridge save six.

On the western end stood the 'Piskey House', possibly Exeter's public conveniences, which was demolished in the 1770s. It was this building that in 1806 Alexander Jenkins noted in his history of Exeter when he wrote of 'a door way and a flight of steps that led to a long vaulted room, commonly called the Pixey or Fairy House'.[96] In 1927 Beatrix Cresswell imagined that it was Mayor Gervase's chapel 'termed the Pixhay, from a confused remembrance of former times, when the pyx (the vessel in which consecrated bread is kept) with the Host was suspended before the altar'.[97]

the existing medieval bridge. The new bridge was opened by March 1778 and it is assumed that the arches of the medieval bridge across the river were taken down shortly afterwards.[94] The remaining nine spans of the bridge were exposed in the 1970s and are now encircled by the traffic crossing the two modern bridges.

Houses on Exe Bridge, drawn in the first half of the nineteenth century.
Demolished in 1883.

The last of these houses built on the medieval bridge was not demolished until the late nineteenth century. W. R. Best, who drew one of the views, wrote that his drawing 'shows the ancient houses overhanging the leat and the north-east part of old Exe Bridge, next St Edmund's Church, from a sketch made by me in 1845. These houses were pulled down in 1883'.[98] In August 1848 three almshouses on the bridge, which had been built in the early sixteenth century, were demolished. As many as 12 arches, extending to as much as 320 feet, were thought to have been covered with buildings.[99] Over the centuries many hundreds of people have lived in these houses known as Old Bridge Street in the early nineteenth century before being renamed Edmund Street. Among these all but forgotten residents was Agnes Griffin, a woman who petitioned the City Chamber in about 1686 that she had kept watch on the bridge by keeping fires during the time of the sickness of Charles II and also during the 'unnatural rebellion' of the Duke of Monmouth in 1685.[100]

4-6. Three views from New Bridge Street of the houses on the medieval bridge. They were drawn in c.1810 possibly by Simon Prout, in c.1830 by M. Rowe, and from New Bridge Street in 1845 by William Rayner Best, architect.

Church of St Edmund, drawn in about 1835.
Demolished for civic improvement, 1972.

The medieval church of St Edmund stood on the medieval bridge. It was reconstructed in 1834 and heavily repaired in 1935. The church was closed in 1956 with one annual service conducted. There was a fire in 1970 and the church was demolished in 1972, with the exception of the tower which was lowered, in the spirit of improvement.

7. Engraving of the medieval church, c.1830, before renovation.

8. Unfinished and undated pencil drawing by John Gendall of the church before restoration in 1834.

Eighteenth-century bridge, drawn in the middle of the nineteenth century.
Demolished in 1904 to increase the flow of traffic.

The medieval bridge was replaced in the 1770s partly because the old bridge was an inconvenient entrance to the city but also, it was claimed, the many arches contributed to flooding during high rains. There was some disagreement: in 1773 a public meeting was held which passed a resolution that 'the bridge was extravagant in its dimensions, of partial use, ill-chosen in its site, and a bridge that must prove a lasting subject of ridicule'.[101] Nevertheless, the foundation stone was laid on 4 October 1770[102] by the Mayor, with the appropriate name of John Floud,[103] and that day the city spent seven pounds and eight shillings in entertainment for the workmen and labourers. There was also a bill for seven pounds and eight shillings for hospitality provided for the constables while nine pounds was laid out for ale given to 'the populace'.[104] A silver plate was engraved and laid under the foundation stone but not long afterwards severe flooding interrupted construction,[105] presumably sending the plate downstream, and mismanagement dragged the work on for eight years. The plate is now in the Royal Albert Memorial Museum. It was later claimed that the bridge cost the city thirty thousand pounds.[106] In 1778 a line was marked on the centre of the bridge to mark the boundaries between the county of Devon and Exeter that was then a county in its own right.[107] The keystone had 'Jehovah' inscribed on it.[108] The bridge was situated further upstream from the medieval bridge to provide direct access to Fore Street. This necessitated the creation of a link road, named New Bridge Street, through the old wall and across the site of the medieval church of All Hallows. The church had been demolished in May 1770 after having been, in the opinion of George Oliver 'an eyesore and nuisance' since the 1650s.[109] Its position on the walls was not advantageous to its safety in the Civil War. The ascent was easier than that of Stepcote Hill, where one Victorian writer noted having seen three horses pulling a single wagon.[110] The new bridge continued in use until 1904. Portland stone from the eighteenth-century bridge was reused in the building of the foundation piers and walls in Barnfield Crescent.[111]

9. Drawing of the eighteenth-century bridge by Edward Ashworth, c.1850. Gas lighting can be seen on the bridge.

10. Drawing by C. J. Bulgin, 1904, of the new bridge. The cornerstone was laid on 23 July 1904 and it was opened on 29 March 1905. A temporary wooden bridge was erected while building work was under way. There had been strenuous efforts made to build a new bridge. In about 1901 H. Tolson argued the case in a pamphlet and claimed that carts had difficulty crossing the bridge when it was frosty or greasy, that the bridge was crowded to capacity with foot passengers, carts and bicycles. He also noted that in St Thomas the approaching streets were too narrow and that funeral processions travelling to the cemetery were often blocked by carts with hay.[112] In 1960 the bridge was named as a contributing cause to the great flood that hit St Thomas and it was demolished in 1973. The first of the two replacement bridges had already been opened four years earlier. New Bridge Street can be seen to the left of the drawing.

11. Photograph of the ceremony laying the cornerstone, 1904.

2. The Carfax, the junction of Fore, High, North and South Streets

For centuries this corner was known as the Carfax, from the Old French *carreforc*, the French Latin *quadrifurcus*, or possibly *Quarte Voies*, the four forks or ways, the place where four streets meet. Oxford is the only other known place in England with this place name.

The Old Conduit, with Fore Street, drawn in 1769.
Demolished in about 1772 in order to improve the flow of traffic.

The Great Conduit, as opposed to the Little Conduit situated near St Lawrence's church in the High Street, was probably rebuilt in the 1530s. This was the main distribution point for water in the city although many wealthier citizens had their own wells. According to the eighteenth-century model by Hedgeland in the Royal Albert Memorial Museum, it was situated at the end of Fore Street just short of the junction. In November 1771 the City Chamber decided, after a year of discussion, to

A VIEW of the SOUTH and EAST SIDES of the OLD CONDUIT in FORE-STREET EXON

12-13. Two similar drawings by or after Mathew Blackamore showing Fore Street from Mary Arches to North Street. The second drawing is dated 1773. The building behind the conduit with the stone cornering was similar to one that stood across from it (see Illustration 39). Both drawings were either by or after Mathew Blackamore, a local drawing master who lived in High Street opposite the Guildhall.[118] The first has the signature of Emmanuel Jeffery, a local artist who worked in Exeter in the 1830s.[119] This may be his copy of a drawing by Blackamore. It is titled 'View of the Old Conduit and part of the Fore Street in Exeter as it stood in the year 1769', dated 23 June 1821 and is possibly a retrospective view to show the conduit before it was dismantled in what was largely assumed to have been its demolition year of 1770. Similar views of the South Gate were particularly popular in Exeter and this drawing may be in that genre. It may also have been that Jeffery merely signed the drawing to express his ownership, he was then only about 15 years old.[120]

award a contract for pulling down the conduit. They also decided to erect a new one a few houses to the east in High Street but dismantled this after a few years and in 1799 built yet another conduit on the eastern side of South Street.[113] The Great Conduit was demolished by 1773 according to one visitor to the city.[114] In 1806 the reasons given by Jenkins in his history of Exeter for its demolition was danger due to traffic congestion.[115] In 1899 the reasons remembered by *The Western Times* for the destruction was 'in consequence of the great inconvenience which occurred by reason of so many people congregating there for the purpose of drawing water'. The notice in the newspaper[116] was prompted by Messrs. Lloyd's, the tobacco, snuff, cigar and cigarette manufacturers located at 76-7 Fore Street,[117] having chosen to mark the Bath and West Show, then being held in the city, by erecting in its window a model of the Conduit. It was constructed of tobacco with running water. The site is now the middle of the traffic junction.

There are significant differences between the two drawings. The style is similar but the lettering of the titles is not. This drawing appears to have either been acquired or copied by Jeffery at the time of the widening of North Street in 1821 which would explain the interest in the corner. The second drawing lacks these buildings and a roofline directly behind the conduit as well as showing a great number of architectural differences in the lamps, doors, windows and one chimney. There is also a gutter for wastewater. Interestingly, the second drawing of 1773 appears to show the conduit with blocked windows unlike that made four years previously. Of course the building may merely have had false windows. There are also some differences indicated in the stonework. It may be that the buildings altered between the times the two drawings were made which would make sense in relation to the conduit given it was just about to be demolished. It is unlikely that either is a copy; each has substantial additions that are unlikely to have arisen while a copy was made. Both drawings may have been copied from an unknown third and original drawing.

14-15. Details of the conduit from the two Blackamore drawings, as 1769, 1773. There are only slight differences in the two depictions. This was one of the most highly decorated public structures in Exeter for centuries and yet few illustrations of it have survived. The style of the two illustrations excludes the vast number of people who were constantly drawing their drinking water from the conduit.

16. Sketch possibly by Mathew Blackamore entitled 'tracing of the Carfax (Quarte-voies) or water conduit which stood near the crossing of High Street with North and South Streets', c.1773.

17. Another view of the conduit, engraved in wood by A. Jenkins after J. Hayman, post 1770.

Corner of Fore and North Streets, drawn in the early nineteenth century.
The two buildings were pulled down in 1882 and 1891.

Number 186 Fore Street, possibly an Elizabethan building, can be seen in a rough drawing by J. C. Griffiths which was engraved in 1873.[121] It, along with Number 185, suffered two fires on 18 January and 27 July 1882. The newspaper report noted of Number 186 that 'very little is left but the shell'.[122] After the second fire it was the only building near the corner. Its replacement was the Brock building, known as Paternoster House,[123] which was built from 1883 to 1884 and still stands. One of the windows from Number 186 is housed in the Royal Albert Memorial Museum.[124] Norcombe, shown above the door, was James Norcombe, mercer and draper. He was there in business in 1828 but had gone by 1844.[125] May & Company, general ironmongers,[126] occupied the building from 1861 to 1881.

18. Drawing by George Townsend, nineteenth century.

19. Photograph of the corner, sometime between 1861 and 1881. St Peter can be seen to the right and North Street is shown before the fire of 1882.

20. Detail of lithograph by James Ackerman, 1884. The outline of Number 187, with St Peter still perched on the corner, can be distinguished on the right. The Brock building had 'two capacious shops in the basement and their contiguous showrooms contain all that is desirable for the exercise of taste and discrimination in the customer'.[127]

North Street, painted in about 1840.

The east side of North Street was demolished from 1969 through the early 1970s for the Guildhall Shopping Centre development.

Until the creation of Queen Street in 1835 the only thoroughfare across the city was South and North Streets. Even so the entrances to North Street were greatly restricted and hampered even eighteenth-century traffic. This resulted in the demolition of the North Gate in June 1769[128] and the widening of the southern end of the street in 1821 by the Improvement Commissioners: years later, in 1876, one Exeter citizen recalled that there was room for only one cart to pass and remembered the congestion regularly caused by a dozen or more carts transporting lime from St Leonard's across the city and through St David's Hill.[129] The street was only ten feet wide in 1819.[130] Improvements continued in 1834: the steep descent into the steep valley, known as the Pit,[131] was lessened by the construction of the Iron Bridge that connected the two sides of the Longbrook valley. Widening took place again in 1898.[132] The row of fifteenth to seventeenth-century town houses that lined North Street survived until the 1970s when they were demolished to make way for the Guildhall Shopping Centre. Many of those seen on the left today are much earlier than their Edwardian facades indicate.

21-2. Two views of North Street by John Gendall, c.1830 to 1840, looking towards the Iron Bridge and St David's Hill.

Number 187 High Street, photographed in about 1889.
Demolished in about 1891 presumably to make way for bigger premises.

Number 187 High Street, the building on the corner with North Street, was originally one building away from that corner. In 1821, according to a report in *Woolmer's Exeter and Plymouth Gazette* that adjoining building, seen in Illustration 12, was demolished.[133] In the late eighteenth century Daniel Floud, linen draper, operated from the building[134] that was about 22 feet along the High Street[135] and by 1819 it housed the West of England Insurance Office.[136] Fifteen years earlier it had been rebuilt and it was noted as having 'stories jutting over each other as they rose upward' with a battlemented roof.[137] The statue of St Peter was the only feature saved in 1821. The Commissioners of Improvement were then widening the entrance to North Street,[138] which was then only ten feet wide,[139] and the *Gazette* reported on 10 February that the building was about to be demolished. The street was widened the 130 feet from High Street to Waterbeer Street. St Peter was removed, placed on the neighbouring building and raised

some six feet from the ground.[140] This building had been occupied by William Cooper, a hatter, in 1772[141] and was the business premises of Holman and Ham, wholesale and retail chemists who were established in the late eighteenth century, until 1891[142] when it was presumably pulled down[143] to make way for the current brick building. It then housed J. Hepworth and Son, clothiers and outfitters, for nearly a hundred years, until 1986, when the building was occupied by the national chain stores Next and latterly Athena.

The statue of St Peter remains a mystery in that it is not known why it was carved and placed overlooking the Carfax. Equally mysterious is how it survived the Reformation, Revolution and Commonwealth. The statue had a high public profile and in the early twentieth century one local newspaper, *Woolmer's Exeter and Plymouth Gazette*, ran a column supposedly penned by the saint. It is most likely that the statue was connected with the cathedral given that its dedication to St Peter. Yet it is clear the Victorians had no certain history of it and many speculated on its origin and history. Beatrix Cresswell, writing in 1927, thought the statue's origin was 'lost in obscurity'.[144] Townsend noted that 'Father Peter – in a niche at the corner of Messrs. Holman and Ham, druggists, – is a medieval image holding the church on his right arm and the bible on his left, and is standing on a black figure supposed to represent Satan. It is not certainly known, but thought to have been at one time in the Cathedral, in the canopy above the Bishop's throne'. The editor of Townsend's works noted that the statue was lower to the ground as did James Cossins in 1876; he remembered that as a child he had been raised to touch it.[145]

How early the statue was there is uncertain or how it could have escaped being destroyed in the sixteenth or seventeenth centuries. It was suggested and quickly refuted that the statue was originally set in the Bishop's Throne.

23. Photograph taken in about 1889.

In 1738 Andrew Brice noted it when he wrote:

By this, where houses, whelving, houses meet,
And vault with beetle-brows a shelving street,
Where stout St Peter on the corner stall,
Props the impending edifice from fall.[146]

In 1821 *Woolmer's Exeter and Plymouth Gazette* could find no 'certain account' of the statue but noted that a theologian had (wrongly) claimed it was not Saint Peter because there were no keys. A week later a letter was sent to the paper from T. W. of Bartholomew Yard claiming that the statue was of Duke Humphries, a man who built St Mary Steps church and that his clothes were intended to suggest his social rank, the church alluded to his building and the book referred to his piety. The paper also noted that a local gentleman wanted it for his garden and, intriguingly, reported that the statue was the remaining one of four that had stood at the junction.[147] Another theory emerged forty-five years later,

in 1867, when it was suggested by one writer that the statue was of St Peter and that it had been erected by the people of Exeter 'in admiration' of Bishop Stapledon who had been murdered in London in 1326. It was explained the bishop's brother had owned the building and granted the rent money from it to pay for remembering him and his family in church, in perpetuity, on the 15th of October.[148] The latest building, still standing, has an empty niche for St Peter.

There were a number of large carved figures that embellished late medieval buildings in Exeter; these included King John's Tavern, the Bear Inn and the Swan Inn. It may have been a feature of late medieval Exeter building; perhaps there was a particular wood carver in Exeter, possibly not even English, responsible for each of these. After at least three centuries the statue was removed from its site in 1983 and given to the Royal Albert Memorial Museum five years later where it remains on view.

Church of St Petrock, High Street, photographed in June 1906.

Buildings removed in 1905 to improve the flow of traffic. The tower was restored the following year.

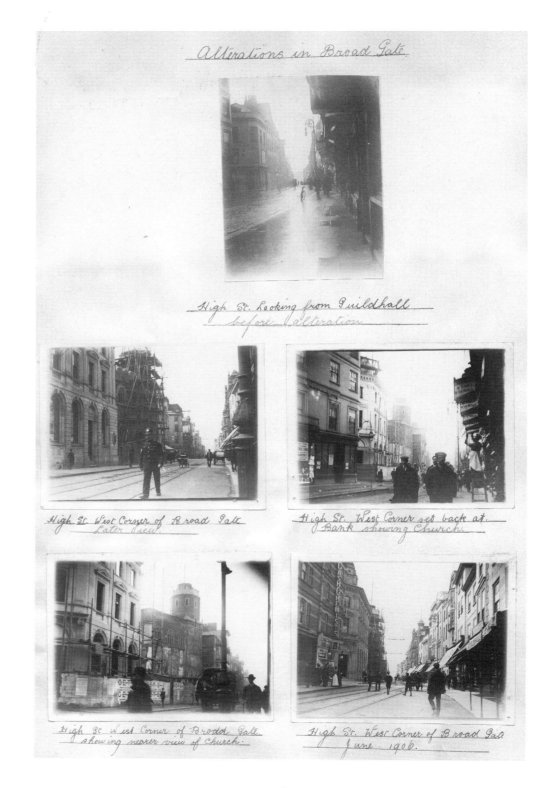

Alterations in Broad Gate

High St. Looking from Guildhall before alteration

High St. West Corner of Broad Gate Later view.

High St. West Corner set back at Bank showing Church.

High St. West Corner of Broad Gate showing nearer view of Church.

High St. West Corner of Broad Gate June 1906.

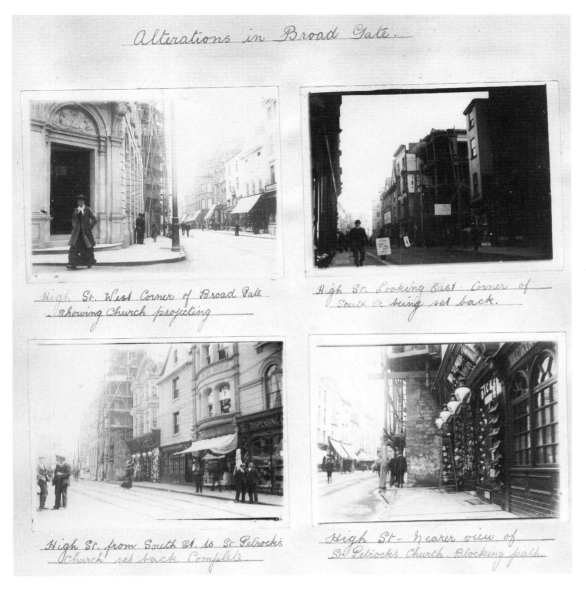

Alterations in Broad Gate.

High St. West Corner of Broad Gate showing Church projecting

High St. Looking East - Corner of South St. being set back.

High St. from South St. to St Petrock's Church set back Complete

High St - nearer view of St Petrock's Church Blocking path

27-35. Series of photographs by Pocknell, June 1906.

The church of St Petrock is not properly on the Carfax or along the High Street nor in Cathedral Close. It is unique among Exeter churches, and churches in general, in that it was entirely surrounded by other buildings with the only tower visible. It is hard to imagine the general view in 1806; the medieval church was then 'obscurely situated and surrounded by houses, that scarce any part of it can be seen except the tower'. Access from the High Street was via a passage way under shop premises.[149] Few of these buildings remain, many were destroyed in the second world war, and others had been redeveloped or removed in 1880 and 1905. In 1906 the parish council restored the tower which had been exposed the year before with the removal of buildings in order to widen High Street for trams. The city council had wanted the tower to be set back but the two sides could not agree financial terms so the tower was merely restored.[150] A plaque on the tower notes that the church had been obscured for two centuries. Edward Pocknell photographed the restoration, a rare example in Exeter of a church building winning an argument over traffic improvement.

Corner of South and High Streets, painted in 1848.
Destroyed when the Luftwaffe bombed the city in 1942.

36. Painting by George Townsend, 1848. At 75 Fore Street, on the corner of South and Fore Street, was the business of James Knight, hosier and haberdasher.[152] The tower of the church of St Petrock can be seen to the left.

Numbers 73 & 74 High Street were the premises of Pasmore, Savery and Pasmore (also known as Pasmore and Wilcocks among other names), 'Manchester warehousemen', from 1828 to 1891. The corner was redeveloped sometime by 1849 if the details of an illustration in *The Illustrated London News* that year are right. In 1891 it was occupied by Holman and Ham, chemists, which relocated from across the street at 187 High Street. Number 73 was subsequently taken over by Lewis Richard Truscott, dining rooms, and then The Fifty Shillings Tailors but Holman and Ham remained in Number 74 until the building was destroyed in the bombing of the city in 1942. Number 1 South Street, to the right of Pasmore & Savery, was occupied by Priscilla Blacking who in 1848 ran an 'Eating House'.[151]

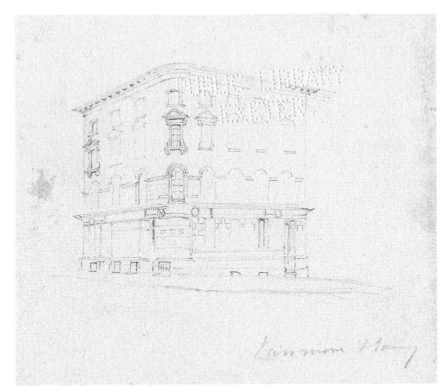
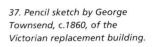

37. Pencil sketch by George Townsend, c.1860, of the Victorian replacement building.

38. Undated pencil sketch by Arthur Glennie, possibly 1828.

Chevalier House, 78-9 Fore Street, painted in about 1850.

The building was destroyed during the Nazi bombing in April 1942.

These two timber-fronted four-storey buildings at numbers 78 and 79 Fore Street, nearly at the top of Fore Street on the south side, could easily be seen from Exeter's great cross ways. The building acquired its name from the ceramic horse and rider placed on the gable end. This ridge tile is like many others that were made in Devon, including Ashburton, Chagford, Dartmouth, Lewtrenchard, Okehampton, Plymouth, Plympton, South Brent, Tavistock and Totnes, as well as in Cornwall and can be seen still on a roof in the Cornish town of Marazion and in the Royal Cornwall Museum in Truro. The tile was popularly, but wrongly, associated with the Royalists through the visits to Exeter by King Charles I and the Prince of Wales during the Civil War,[153] hence the name Chevalier or sometimes Cavalier given to the house. The tradition of such tiles is much older.[154] Wine and spirit merchants used the two buildings from the late nineteenth century to 1923. These seventeenth-century buildings were threatened with demolition in 1929 when Woolworth's, then situated in an adjoining building, wanted the land to expand but the city council was able to borrow the money to buy the buildings.[155] Shortly after this an American visitor was told the story and remarked that it demonstrated 'under what destructive pressure these ancient structures still exist'.[156] The buildings were saved through the intervention of the city council but only for a further thirteen years: unfortunately the Luftwaffe bombing in 1942 destroyed both buildings.

The cavalier and his horse were perched high overlooking the Carfax for three centuries after the civil war with which he was associated before finally falling to ground. Presumably he still lies underneath, in fragments or dust, in the rubble upon which the current building stands. Of all of Exeter's lost iconic images this horse and rider would be the most easily replaced.

39. Detail of a photograph of Fore Street with the Chevalier Building, 1893.

40. Detail of a photograph of the chevalier, taken in about 1930, with the corner of High Street and North Street visible.

41. (Opposite)
Drawing by John Gendall, c.1850. On the back is written, possibly by Thomas Shapter who wrote The History of the Cholera in Exeter in 1832 and who gave the drawing to Exeter City Library, 'left hand side below South Street, vide History of Cholera'. The drawing was presumably used for the engraving.

3. South Street

South Street was one of the city's principal four streets, but considerably narrower until the first years of the nineteenth century. It was lined from Southgate to the Carfax with significant private and public buildings.

42. Pencil and gouache by John Gendall, probably 1834, in which the artist depicted the widening of South Street. Conduits were known for their raucous atmospheres: one Victorian writer noted that 'the vicinity of the conduit was the scene of many amusing episodes. There were frequent quarrels as to right of precedency in the drawing of water; and often the transactions were characterised by broken heads, as well as by broken pitchers'.[164] Another Victorian remembered that twenty to thirty people could be waiting for their water and that it would take half an hour to fill a bucket or pitcher. He thought the reason for its popularity was that the water was considered the best for making tea and pea soup.[165]

Conduit, South Street, drawn in about 1834.

Demolished in 1834 in order to widen South Street.

The Conduit was begun in February 1800[157] as a successor to the Great Conduit located uphill at the junction of Fore Street with South and North Streets. The Great Conduit had served the needs of a large population and it had been difficult finding an appropriate location for its replacement. After some uncertainty the chosen location was in front of the South Street entrance to the Vicars Choral. It was approximately seventeen feet long and nine feet wide.[158] However, the building barely lasted thirty years. Starting in 1830 South Street was 'improved' through attempts to widen the street for the ease of traffic.[159] These improvements were being made shortly before the outbreak of cholera in Exeter in 1832[160] but the severity of the disease in Exeter must have pushed efforts on. Porches were removed and buildings (see below) were pulled back, in some cases more than 24 feet from the street.[161] While this work was being done Gendall sketched four workers on the roofs and three ladders in. The Conduit was removed as part of these efforts sometime after May 1834,[162] possibly as late as November.[163]

43-4. Two views by George Townsend, probably retrospectives, of the conduit. On the back of the drawing below he noted 'this was one of the not too numerous city water supplies of the last century, the stream not being larger than that afforded by a 3/4 inch pipe. The conduit was a school of patience, the tedium of waiting being occasionally diversified by the excitement of a pugilistic encounter for precedence'.

King John Tavern, 100 South Street, drawn in 1834.

Partly demolished in 1834 in order to widen South Street.

A late medieval building[166] located on the west side of the upper end of South Street directly opposite Little Stile. It housed a Roman Catholic chapel by 1773 if not 1745.[167] In 1806 Alexander Jenkins wrote in his history of Exeter that 'King John's Palace' had been recently altered by its owner, the cabinet maker Henry Flashman.[168] In 1815 the building reopened as The King John Tavern and Commercial Coffee House and offered, among other things, mock turtle to homes in the villages around Exeter but two years later the establishment closed.[169] In 1835 the city's Improvement Commissioners paid Ann Powning, the widow of a local builder, the sum of £310 as compensation for trimming back her property: the work seems to have comprised rebuilding the front in

order to take it back some fifteen and a half feet from the street. Three years later the tavern, later known as the King George Tavern,[170] was listed as including a court, stables and back buildings.[171] In a *Prize essay on the history and antiquities of Exeter by our own board school boy* the writer somewhat humorously wrote it 'was shut up about thirty years ago as the house was wanted to improve the street'. By the late 1870s the building housed George Knott, tailor, and the Exeter Conservative Association.[172] Part of the site of the building was revealed in 1881 during construction work and it was thought that some of the carved wood had been kept in storage since 1854.[173] It was at this time that Richard Lloyd & Sons, tobacco, snuff and cigar manufacturers, destroyed the remaining part of the building in order to build a tobacco factory.[174] The firm continued there until 1924 when it became the premises of F. W. Woolworth.[175]

45-6. Two pencil sketches by John Gendall, probably 1834, of work being undertaken on the tavern. The corner with High and Fore Street can be seen in the distance as can the statue of St Peter. These may be the sketches referred to by Robert Dymond in 1880 as having belonged to Thomas Shapter.[176]

47. Drawing by John Gendall, c.1834, of the staircase.

48. Lithograph by Edward Ashworth, probably based on Gendall's drawing. The front of the building, shown to the right, can be seen in the other drawings being dismantled.

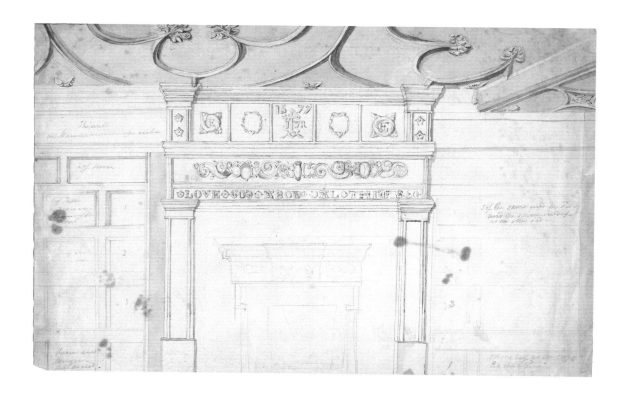

49-50. Two drawings by John Gendall of the interior of King John's Tavern, c.1834. The motto above the fireplace is 'Love God Above All Others' with the date 1577 and the initials JWR.

Church of St George, painted in the mid-nineteenth century.
Demolished in 1843 in order to widen South Street.

The medieval church of St George was situated near the tavern but further down South Street. In 1806 Alexander Jenkins noted it as having been in good repair[177] but in the 1830s a row of buildings from the corner with Fore Street were set back leaving the church intruding into the pavement. At the top of South Street the buildings were set back thirteen and a half feet.[178] The rector resisted moves to demolish the church: he offered to take down part of the building if he was allowed twice the land at the back.[179] The church was demolished upon his death in 1843. Part of it was revealed following bomb damage in the second world war and subsequently moved across South Street where it can be seen today. The Townsend depicted was probably George Townsend, a currier.[180]

51. Undated painting by George Townsend of the church of St George.

Russell & Company, 23-4 South Street, at the corner with Bear Street, drawn in 1881.

Demolished in 1881 to make way for a new church.

Site of the Bear Inn, an ancient building which in 1806 Alexander Jenkins noted in his history of Exeter as having been owned by the Priory of Plympton.[181] It was supposed that the building acquired its great statue of a bear because it was the symbol of the priory. Jenkins noted that the inn was 'built of free stone, of excellent gothic workmanship, decorated with fretwork panels'. But he also noted that they were in a 'ruinous state' and were pulled down to make room for a dwelling house and office for Mr Robert Russell.[182] Russell operated his transport business from there and lived in the adjoining building. One Exeter resident recollected that in the early nineteenth century South Street was so narrow that

Russell's wagons had to partially unload at the top of the street.[183] In 1805 he was found guilty of creating a public nuisance in leaving his unloaded wagons in South Street.[184] The firm continued there until 1844 by which time it was known as Russell & Whitmarsh.[185] In the 1870s it housed George Cooper, wholesale stationer and L. & M. Tole, milliners and librarians.[186] The other businesses, indicated in the drawing, were those of Musgrave Bickford, auctioneer, and William Trenchard, umbrella manufacturer.[187] The buildings only appeared to have last some 80 years: the row of buildings were pulled down to build the Roman Catholic church of the Sacred Heart. During the building work at the end of 1882 workmen found a statue, minus its head and shoulders, made of Beer stone with outer vestments made of needlework. It was presumed to have come from the time when Plympton Priory owned the site.[188] Also, a window frame from the Bear Inn was incorporated within the church fabric.[189]

52. Drawing by George Townsend, 3 May 1881, which was most like made shortly before the buildings were demolished.

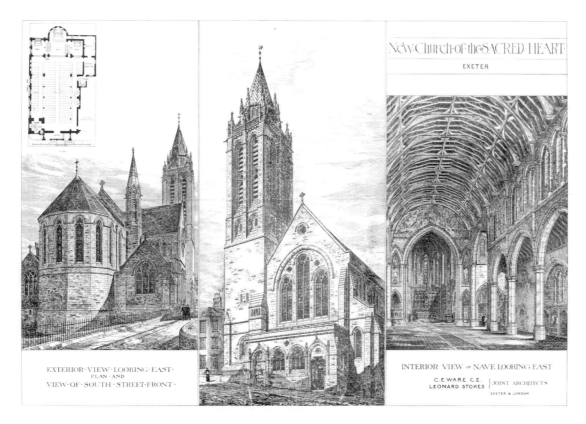

53. Wood engraving showing the newly-built Church of the Sacred Heart, 1881.

54. Drawing by George Townsend of a row of buildings further down South Street, just below the Baptist Chapel, between Bear Street and Palace Gate, mid nineteenth century. The numbers of the buildings have since been changed. In 1853 Thomas Dare was a green grocer and John Tucker a broker.[190]

Corner of Palace Gate and South Street, as painted in 1875 and 1876.
Redeveloped in 1876.

55-6. Two drawings by George Townsend, 1875 and 1876, showing the reconstruction of the buildings at the corner of South Street and Palace Gate, with the replacement of the corner building, the raising of one storey of a building in Palace Gate and the renovation of several others.

The site may have been owned by Plympton Priory in the thirteenth century[191] and later acquired by the City Chamber.[192] The gateway and house were demolished in 1812 and the upper part of the street widened.[193] In 1875 Edward Peters acquired Number 32 South Street and this presumably began the renovation.[194] For more than 25 years the Peters family had already been

operating their grocery business on that corner.[195] In 1871 William Peters, tea dealer and grocer, occupied Number 32 with his wife Emily, their three children, one assistant, two apprentices and two servants. The other firms, noted in the illustration for 1875 but which were gone the following year, were Richard Isaacs, boot closer, who lived at Number 30 with his wife, three children and

one servant, George H. Coles, a poulterer from Topsham, who lived at Number 31 with his wife Ann, one daughter and a servant, and William Davey, currier and land owner, who lived at Number 33 with his wife, two sons and one servant.[196] The firm, called Peters & Hamlin, were only there until the mid 1880s.[197] The buildings were destroyed during the bombing of Exeter in 1942 and the site redeveloped in about 1958 by Exeter City Council.

Holy Trinity church and South Gate, drawn in 1819.

The two buildings were demolished as part of civic improvements in 1819.

The South Gate was rebuilt between 1410 and 1420[198] and it served as the city's prison until 1819. Debtors were housed in rooms in the arch. On 13 November 1818 one individual with the surname of Holmyard was the last prisoner to be executed. Years later an observer remembered him being transported on a cart, with his coffin beside him, to the gallows then in Magdalen Street. He had been convicted of forgery.[199] In 1818 the church committee of Holy Trinity parish decided to pull down the church tower, which stood inside of the gate and impeded traffic, and rebuild the medieval church on

57. Drawing by William Rayner Best, architect, of the inside face of the gate, nineteenth century. Best noted 'a worthy and respected citizen, Mr John Samuel Ramson, now hale and vigorous at 96, tells me that he remembers purchasing at a baker's shop between South Gate and the archway. The man's name was Cross'.

nearly the same site. This was started the following year and the foundation stone was laid on 24 June.[200] The South Gate prison was also demolished in 1819. Henry Ellis remembered that 'this prison was of great strength and was one of the lingering remnants of the feudal times. It abutted on the town walls and with its round battle-mounted keep and look holes presented a very picturesque appearance but being dark and loathsome it was pronounced by the philanthropist [John] Howard to be the worst prison he had visited in the kingdom'.[201] In 1861 the historian George Oliver wrote that he rejoiced in November 1818 when he saw the keystone of the

58. Wash by Robert Dymond titled 'View of Trinity Church and South Gate Exeter from South Street', March 1819.

archway fall to the ground: 'Thank God!' he later wrote.[202] The inmates were sent to the new prison that was erected on what would be later the site of the Rougemont Hotel in Queen Street. The parishioners had intended to note on the foundation stone that the inmates of the South Gate prison, with which the church was entwined, left prison on the same day but logistics delayed their leaving for another five days and the added

59. Drawing by Robert Dymond titled 'View of Southgate Exeter from Magdalene Street', January 1820. Henry Ellis noted in his diary that the buildings to the left were left untouched by the taking down of Southgate.[203]

line was not inscribed. In 1806 Jenkins noted that not only did the church tower project into the gate and narrow the passageway but that it was 'rendered still worse by an arched building adjoining the tower'.[205] The church and gate were nearly one building in two parts and the demolition of one made it necessary to pull down the other. Thus in 1819 ended the curious arrangement where for centuries the city's prison and one of its parish churches were so closely connected. The new church was opened on Christmas day 1820 but was still being furnished several years later.[206]

60. Pencil sketch entitled 'old court behind south side of Trinity Church', dated 6 September 1875. Part of the Southgate Hotel is situated on this site.

Butchers' Row, drawn in the early nineteenth century.

A narrow street of houses which was demolished from the 1830s through to c.1966.

Butchers' Row was the north end of Smythen Street and ran parallel with Fore Street nearly to South Street. In the early 1830s there were 29 butcher stalls[206] and in 1838 the row comprised nearly 70 buildings, including the Golden Fleece public house.[207] This was a few years after the building of the Lower Market on the site of some demolished buildings in the Row.[208] In 1806 Alexander Jenkins, in his history of Exeter, considered the buildings 'low and mean' but wrote that 'the knights of the steel reside in a sort of community among themselves'.[209] The waste water from the South Street Conduit passed through Butchers' Row and somewhat cleansed the street as it passed through to Stepcote Hill to the leat. The Lower Market was started on 14 April 1835 and opened in an unfinished state on 10 December 1836 to a design by Charles Fowler.[210] It was destroyed just over a hundred years later in 1942. The moving of the market from Butchers' Row was a great controversy in Exeter but

61. Detail of pencil drawing titled 'Smithen Street, Exeter' by Arthur Glennie, possibly 1827.

not over the importance of saving buildings. Henry Ellis remembered that because of 'the increase of population and traffic, with stage coaches and vehicles of every description (the Great Western Road being through the street) the market was found to be very inconvenient if not dangerous'.[211] Until 1833 the only way for carts into the market from Fore Street had been under St John's Bow.[212] Remains of three of the last buildings in Butchers' Row were still standing as late as 1966.[213]

62. Drawing by E. Jeffery, possibly 1820s, of the same buildings.

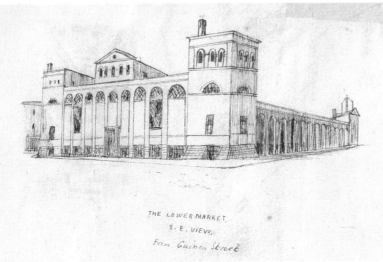

THE LOWER MARKET.
S. E. VIEW.
From Guinea Street

63. Drawing of the Lower Market attributed to A. G. Junaig, 1874. It was built on the site of some of Butchers' Row and on the day the foundation stone was laid, 4 April 1835, an inscription was placed in a glass bottle by the mayor.[214]

4. Cathedral Close

Nearly a city within a city: the Close was an enclave of the church separate from the jurisdiction of the city authorities and from the thirteenth to nineteenth centuries enclosed by substantial gates which effectively sealed it from the city at night.

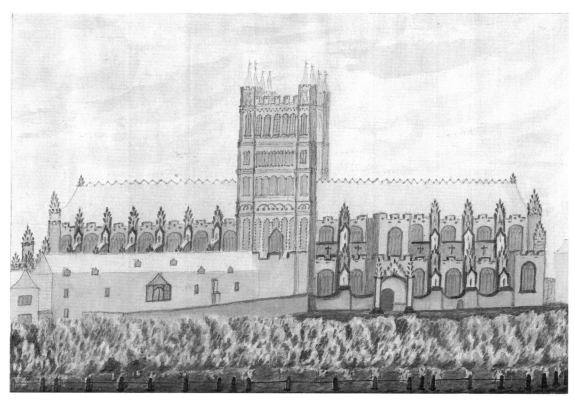

64. Undated watercolour by Elizabeth Tremlett viewing the north side of the cathedral. The line of trees may be the elms planted in the eighteenth century that were noted by Andrew Brice in his Gazeteer of 1774 and the window may be that associated with Henry VII. It is (erroneously) noted on the picture that this is a view of 'Exeter Cathedral and Treasury House, the latter taken down in the year 1797'.

The Treasurer's House, also known as the Treasury House, possibly drawn in about 1820.
Demolished in two phases in the late eighteenth and early nineteenth centuries to improve the Cathedral Yard.

Surprisingly one of the better known of Exeter's lost buildings, particularly to visitors, because the former roofline can still be seen on the cathedral exterior wall. Located on the north side of the cathedral on what is now laid to lawn, the Treasurer's House may have been built as early as the fourteenth century. Its most famous use was to house Henry VII when he came to view the rebels who had besieged Exeter in 1497. A window was enlarged, and trees cut down in the close, to improve his viewing. The building was intended to be used as a workhouse and house of correction in 1652.[215] In the eighteenth century it appears to have become largely redundant as the bishop acted as treasurer and the building was rented out. It was demolished in two phases. The first was in the late eighteenth century, possibly in 1797 as indicated in the painting, when part of it near the tower was taken down.[216] Then in 1820 it was offered to the Dean and Chapter on the demise of

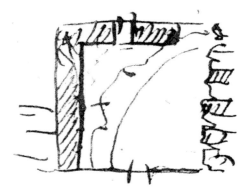

65. Sketch by Thomas Turner of
the Treasurer's House, 1820.
Presumably the smaller building
was the stable and the row were
the out buildings sited along the
cathedral.

the last tenant. On 12 February 1821 a faculty, or license, for demolition was granted[217] and the 'dwelling house with offices (outbuildings), stables, coach house and garden ground'[218] must have been pulled down immediately, 'for the improvement of the Cathedral Yard',[219] given the building materials were sold on 28 March. Among them was a 'large window with shutters', possibly that which had been built for Henry VII, sold for one pound and eleven shillings.[220] A few days later it was noted in the *Flying Post* that the materials were to be removed immediately. Oddly enough, in early February it was observed in *Woolmer's Exeter and Plymouth Gazette* that the Cathedral Yard was 'a beautiful miniature of pastoral scenery, rarely seen in the heart of a populous city; a flock of sheep and lambs are at pasture in the newly-made green on the north side of the cathedral'.[221] The building stretched from the North Tower to the east end and was one of several which were removed from a corner formerly fairly tight with buildings: alongside the cobbles which lead to Southernhay on the right hand side there were several other houses. Further to the west of the building was the Charnel House, located between it and Broadgate, and demolished in 1549. Upon demolition shrubs were planted at the east end and the ground put to lawn after one hundred cart loads of soil were brought in: presumably the centuries of burial in the ground around the Treasurer's House had raised the level of the soil substantially.[222]

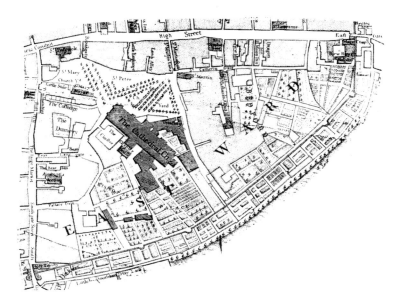

66. Detail of the map of the city by John Rocque, 1744, which shows the number of buildings formerly in the Close.

Church of St Mary Major, drawn in 1823.

Demolished in 1865 in order to build a new church.

The medieval church of St Mary Major stood near the West Front of the cathedral. The tower was lowered in 1581 and 1768. Demolition began in July 1865 and a new building was finished in 1867. Its architect, Edward Ashworth, claimed that he had not intended to destroy the existing building but wrote 'why this arrangement was not carried out . . . I cannot explain'. Several of the Vicars Choral buildings were also demolished to build the new church.[223] This Victorian building was itself taken down barely a hundred years later, in 1971, as part of efforts to improve the view of the cathedral. In 1501 the weather vane of the church disturbed the sleep of Catherine of Aragon who was staying at the Deanery. The princess was travelling from Spain to London for her marriage to the Prince of Wales and insisted that the weather vane be pulled down; workmen duly climbed the steeple at night during the fierce storm to remove it.

67. Pencil sketch by John Harris, 31 July 1823.

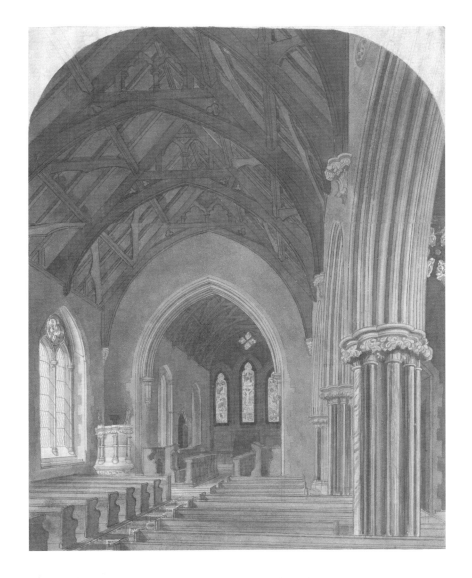

68. Undated interior view by
Charles Ashworth, sometime after
1865, of his father's church.

69. Undated sketch by George
Townsend of a view of the
medieval church from the
cathedral. He noted that the
buildings to the left were
removed at the time the church
was rebuilt.

The Post Office, Cathedral Cloisters, drawn as in 1791.
Pulled down in 1819.

Exeter's post office was located in a small building on the side of the West Front from 1791 to 1803 when it moved to Gandy Street. Nine years later it moved to Bedford Lane[224] and later opened in its premises in Queen Street. In 1853 Dr Thomas Shapter recalled he had been told that some 60 to 70 years before the Post Office was run by a young girl; he said at a soiree of the Exeter Literary Society that it was kept by 'an old gentleman who was past all duty' and that 'the only person who received and stamped and delivered letters was one little girl, and

70. Drawing by George Townsend, possibly drawn in about 1870 from a print dated 1791.

even she was not occupied more than an hour or two a day'.[225] A generation later James Cossins, in 1876, recollected being told by an acquaintance that he remembered only two clerks worked at the post office and one woman carried a basket in which to deliver letters.[226] The building had been the home of Zachary Dashwood in the 1660s and by a number of clerics, merchants and gentry in the eighteenth century until it became the post office. The crenellated wall in front of the house may have been part of the cloister wall.[227] The building was demolished as part of John Kendall's improvements in 1819 when buildings were being removed from the cloisters.[228]

71. Drawing by George Townsend, 3 August 1871, of the adjoining house. This was a seventeenth-century building that in the 1660s was home to John Loosemore, the famous organ builder. It was demolished in 1871.[229]

The Broad Gate, drawn in 1823.
Demolished from 1824 to 1825 for traffic improvements.

Rebuilt medieval gate that was originally constructed in the thirteenth century.[230] The building accommodated members of the cathedral work staff, in 1815 this included the cathedral's Scavenger and Lamplighter.[231] The gate was the only entrance wide enough into Cathedral Yard to accommodate coaches. In November 1822 the Commissioner of Improvement decided to pull down the gate and for the next two years discussed it with the Dean and Chapter.[232] In March 1824 the owner of the Clarence Hotel petitioned the Commissioners to upgrade the entrance into Cathedral Yard on the grounds that there had recently been a serious accident.[233] This had involved the Bristol and Bath Coach: the coach had come into contact with the gate, broke into two halves with the horses and pole racing off to the Hotel and the coach with its passengers was left behind at the gate. Only minor injuries were suffered by the driver and guard when they were thrown from their seats.[234] His petition was successful and moves were undertaken to take down the gate. Local dissent continued but demolition began on 28 December 1824 and the gateway was reopened for use by carriages on the 28th of February.[235] In the interim they had used Cathedral Yard via Catherine Street then known as Martin Street.[236] When the gate was being demolished it was observed that the stone from the upper part of the gate 'appear to abound in marine productions'.[237] Henry Ellis noted that the demolition was regrettable given the gate was a 'relic' of cathedrals but it 'was most dangerous and accidents frequently occurred from it'.[238] In 1826 the Dean and Chapter placed an inscribed stone, which is still there, to note where the gate had stood.[239] In 1833 houses adjoining the Broad Gate were pulled down in order to rebuild them further back and widen the entrance into Cathedral Yard. It led to the corner house with Fore Street being later removed and others also being rebuilt as far as the National and Provident Bank building that was also rebuilt.[240]

72. Ink sketch by John Harris, 1823, from High Street into Cathedral Close. The church of St Mary Major can be seen in the distance.

73. Copper line engraving by F. Nash after J. Farington, 1822, from his drawing made a decade before.

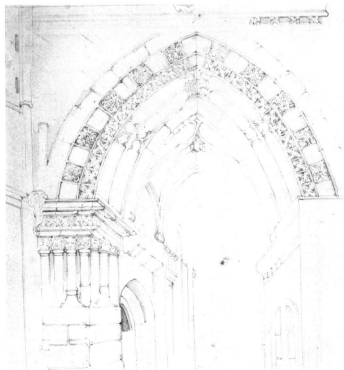

74. Detail of unsigned pencil sketch, c.1824.

Oriel window in Thomas Elyot's house, as drawn in the late eighteenth century.
Removed to the Bishop's Palace.

The Oriel window was in the former home of Thomas Elyot, a local customs official, which was between Broadgate and St Petrock's church. The window was on the back of the building which had its front on High Street. The window was inserted into the Bishop's Palace in the middle of the nineteenth century.

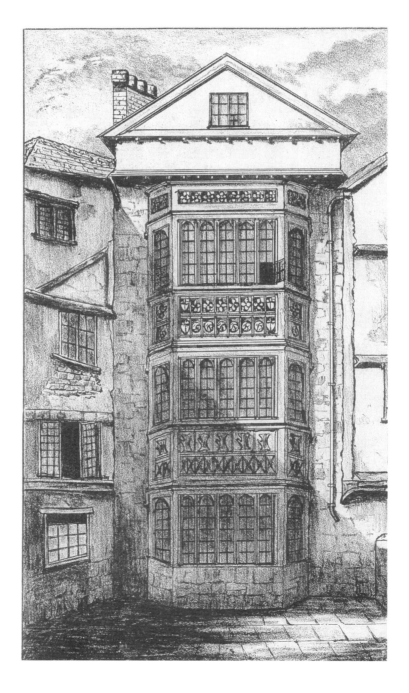

75. Lithograph by W. C. Featherstone, 1839.

Globe Hotel, photographed in about 1920.
Destroyed in the blitz, 1942

The hotel was formerly known as the Globe Tavern and stood in Cathedral Yard adjacent to the church of St Petrock on the one side and to Elyot's house on the other. The hotel comprised a four-storied Georgian building on the right with a lower earlier building of three floors on the south side. On the left hand side was Little Stile, a footpath leading to South Street and on the left was a second right of way through the hotel. It had been the home of the Northmore family in the seventeenth century[241] following which, by 1676 at least,[242] it became a tavern. In the eighteenth century it was known for cockfighting.[243] The hotel was a general rendezvous point for the city's popular 5th of November celebrations in Cathedral Close. The meetings of the country's first bee-keeping society were held there for ten years from 1797.[244] The hotel was destroyed during the Nazi bombing of Exeter in 1942.

76. Photograph of the Globe Hotel taken in about 1920.

College of the Vicars Choral, drawn in the nineteenth century.
Demolished for sense of improvement and destroyed through bombing in the nineteenth and twentieth centuries.

The buildings of the College of the Vicars Choral, situated between the Deanery and South Street, were mostly demolished between 1850 and 1893. Ashworth removed some of the buildings when he rebuilt the church of St Mary Major. The main hall survived until the second world war when it was destroyed during the blitz.

77. Pencil sketch possibly by Arthur Glennie of the college buildings, early nineteenth century.

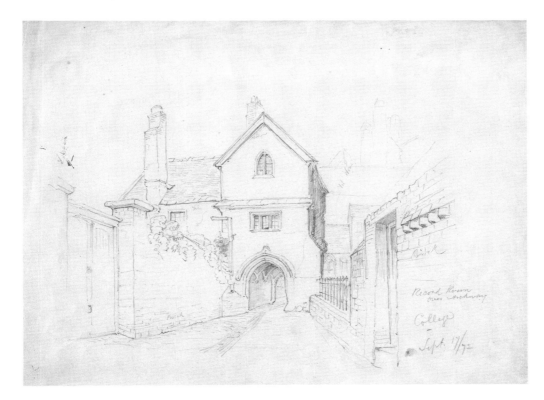

78. Pencil sketch by George Townsend entitled 'Record room over archway', 17 September 1872.

79. Drawing by K. M. Clarke looking towards South Street, 1890.

5. Goldsmith Street

Goldsmith Street is all but forgotten except by those who knew it before the development of the Guildhall Shopping Centre altered it from one of the main ways through the city into a walkway.

80. Drawing by William Rayner Best, architect, nineteenth century.

210 High Street, the corner of Goldsmith Street and High Street, drawn in the late nineteenth century.

Demolished in 1880 in order to improve traffic flow.

The building on the east corner of Goldsmith Street with High Street was removed in 1879. It may have been built as early as 1618 and was up to 8 feet in width.[245] The edition to the print noted that the artist had written 'the old house and shop of Mr George Huggins, druggist, which hung on to the church was purchased and pulled down in 1879 to widen the street' and added 'On a portion of the site of this shop a temporary structure known as the Shanty was put up by Messrs Wheaton.' Wheaton was located further east down High Street at the corner with Queen Street from 1895 to 1928. The building had been the business premises first of George Huggins from the 1820s and later of Henry Huggins, both listed as either druggists or chemists, until it was demolished.[246]

81. Sketch by James Crocker, about 1879.

Allhallows church, Goldsmith Street, as photographed in 1906.
Demolished in 1906 for civic improvements.

In 1658 the small medieval church of Allhallows on Goldsmith Street escaped being demolished through the actions of a local medical doctor but had no such benefactor three centuries later when it finally was destroyed. By the end of the nineteenth century it already had an erratic history: in the 1760s the tower was lowered, and for a short while, from 1807 to 1822, services were discontinued[247] but the church was given a new vibrancy with a later rector. One Exeter resident went so far as noting in his diary that the church had been closed for over a century.[248] However, in 1880 the *Exeter Flying Post* reported there were council and parish meetings regarding a plan of demolition. At one meeting a parishioner stated that the proposal actually dated back to 1820 on the grounds of the inconvenience

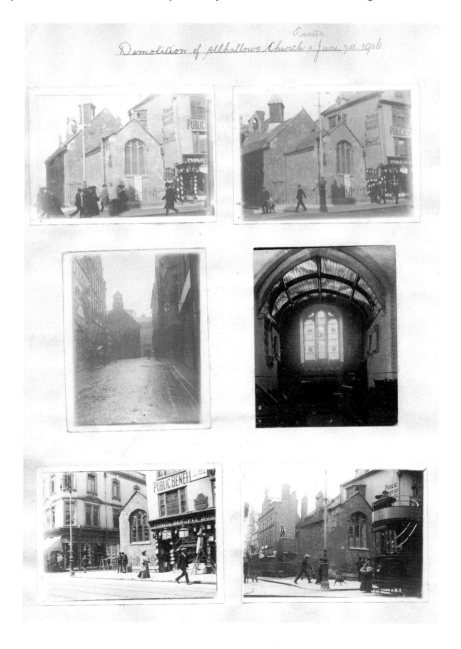

and danger to the public. He himself claimed to have witnessed the death of a young girl caused by traffic. He said 'whenever there was a block in the street it was the occasion of an amount of bad language that could not but excite regret . . . the improvement was desirable from a sanitary point of view' and advised 'Go into any of the old houses in the narrow part of the street and they would experience a most offensive smell of sewer gas'. In 1880 of the 50 tenements in the parish only eleven families, some 50 people, attended services at the church.[249] At the end of that century, claiming the powers of the Exeter Corporation Act of 1900, the city council once again sought the church's destruction. Two reasons were given; firstly, the church was unnecessary because there were insufficient residents in the parish to support the building, and secondly, Goldsmith Street was dangerous to traffic owing to its narrowness. The Dean and Chapter gave their consent for the demolition of the building with several conditions, one of which was that subsequent use would not be unseemly, irreverent or liable to cause a scandal.[250] In the first week of June 1906 the church was demolished and Edward Pocknell photographed the event.

82-92. A series of photographs of the church, 7 June 1906, by Edward Pocknell. His photographs show the demolition from the church before work began and to where it has been reduced to a pile of stones.

Goldsmith Street, as painted in 1938.
The west side of the street was all but demolished in the 1970s.

93. Drawing by Dennis Flanders, 1938, looking towards High Street and the cathedral with Higher Market on the left. The level of the pedestrian way was raised in 1970s.

Goldsmith Street was not destroyed by bombs in the second world war but through the redevelopment of the area in the 1970s. Goldsmith Street was one of the two main entrances into Higher Market from the 1830s until the 1970s. The Bull Hotel, seen to the right at Number 13 Goldsmith Street, was also demolished. It had been in existence by 1715[251] and in 1838 included a brew house, cellars, stables, shed and court.[252] The entrance to the court can be seen to the right. The hotel continued until 1948 when the building was taken over by St John's Ambulance.

94. Anonymous nineteenth-century drawing of the east side of Goldsmith Street looking from the High Street towards Paul Street with the church of St Paul in the distance.

95. Lithograph by Henry Besley, c.1860, looking towards High Street.

6. Queen Street

The only means of crossing Exeter was through North and South Streets until the creation of Queen Street (initially called Higher Market Street and renamed Queen Street in 1839) in the late 1830s. The purpose of Queen Street was to give better access to the Higher Market, one of the city's two new markets built in the 1830s, and to connect with the newly-built New North Road. That building was begun on 8 May 1835 and opened in a grand ceremony on 24 July 1838 at six in the morning by the mayor and receiver who were attended by the local police.[253]

96. Drawing by John Gendall, c.1840, on the back is written, possibly by Thomas Shapter, the Exeter doctor, who gave the painting to Exeter City Library 'on right hand side below Gandy Land the house to the right (Civet Cat) was the old Mayoralty House refaced trans[?formed] of the old house within'. When Higher Market opened there was not yet an easy way through from the High Street and Numbers 220 to 222 were demolished to create the new street. Number 220 was possibly the entrance to the Swan Tavern, Number 221 was owned by Thomas Knott, a druggist,[254] and Number 222 belonged to one Mrs Higgs. Houses in Paul Street were also removed and the road crossed through a private garden to reach the new city prison.[255] A carriage is shown in the illustration coming from Queen Street.

219-28 High Street, as painted in the mid-nineteenth century.
Some of the buildings were demolished and others extensively renovated.

The main illustration shows the row of townhouses that made up 219-228 High Street, with the newly-created Queen Street.

219 High Street, situated at the western corner of Queen Street, was occupied in 1851 by Joseph Wippell, woollen draper, and his wife, their five children, one assistant and two servants.[256] In 1847 he was described as 'mercer and church decorator'.[257]

223 High Street, situated at what became the eastern corner of Queen Street, was occupied by John Collins, a straw plait manufacturer, in 1851.[258] The building was demolished sometime in the middle of the nineteenth century.[259] From at least 1867 until 1928 it housed five consecutive firms of either stationers or booksellers including Wheaton. Boots, the chemists, occupied it from 1929 until 1958.[260] The building was demolished in about 1970[261] and the current building erected in 1973.[262]

224 High Street, was the premises of Robert G. Visick, a chemist originally from Kingsbridge, from 1842 to 1854. In 1851 he employed two apprentice chemists and lived above the shop with them and his wife, their five children and three servants.[263] It became the premises of James Sweet Cape, chemist in the 1880s and Henry William Harris, another chemist, by 1890. It was subsequently taken over by Wheaton and then Boots.[264]

225-6 High Street, a pair of timber-fronted houses. In 1851 Number 225 was the business premises of Mary A. Luxon, baby linen manufacturer, who resided there with her female assistant Jane Rawling.[265] Number 226 has

thought to have been built in 1567 by Thomas Prestwood, a merchant. From 1781 it was home to Robert Trewman who printed the *Exeter Flying Post* in the building. Several other newspapers were also printed there. The building was heavily restored in 1907[266] and, like Numbers 225 and 227, rebuilt behind a restored façade in 1971.

227 High Street, another timber-fronted merchant house, was built in the middle of the seventeenth century. From at least the late 1820s until 1842 it was the premises of William George, hatter and hosier.[267] By 1851 it was occupied by Charles Collins, a London tailor, along with his wife, their seven children and one servant in one half and by Maria Crediford, linen draper, three additional linen drapers, one milliner and a servant in the other.[268] But for nearly a hundred years the building was the business premises of J. & G. Ross, tailors; they were there from 1852 until 1951.[269] The building was greatly restored in 1878 and nearly a hundred years later its façade was retained to partly hide a new building.

228 High Street, The Mayoralty House, the *Civet Cat*, at the corner with Gandy Street, was closely associated with the Guildhall. On the building can be seen the letters 'The Civet'. It was leased by the Corporation in 1733 and then purchased from John Heath, the Exeter judge, in 1759 for £600. The building was used for the mayor's entertaining including Assize judges. It was sold in 1815[270] and was subsequently used as commercial premises for more than a dozen milliners and dressmakers in 1851 as well as by Samuel Star, a toy merchant. Grant Brothers, importers and dealers in foreign and fancy goods, were there in the 1870s and 1870s. It was then known as 'The Civet Cat Fancy Warehouse'.[271] The building was replaced in 1980.

97. Drawing by George Townsend, c.1839, of the front door of the Swan. Known as the Swan Inn/Hotel/Tavern, it was popular in the eighteenth century and had as its main room The Snuggery in which was an oak chair, raised some two feet from the ground, with the words 'God Save the King' painted on it. A chairman would sit and demand that later guests removed their hats or leave.[272] In 1773, just a few years after the Royal Clarence was built, one visitor compared the two establishments. He wrote of the Swan that 'the behaviour of the domestics was English and the eatables and drinkables as good as an Englishman could wish for'. But of the Clarence, 'a house of the bon-ton', he observed 'if ceremonious servility and foppish manners can please a downright Englishman he may meet enough of it there'; all the food was, he wrote, 'served in fricassee or soup'.[273] The Swan was demolished in stages in the 1830s for access to the new market.

Queen Street between Northernhay and Upper Paul Street, as depicted for 1860.
Redeveloped in 1865.

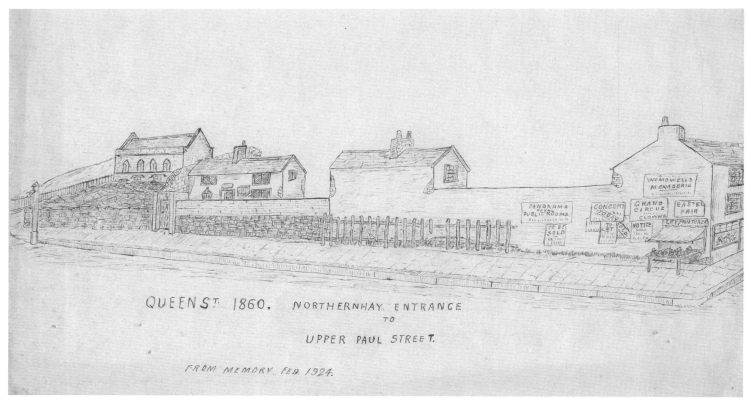

QUEEN ST. 1860. NORTHERNHAY. ENTRANCE TO UPPER PAUL STREET.

FROM MEMORY. FEB. 1924.

98. Retrospective pen sketch by F. Algar, of Queen Street in 1860 as drawn in February 1924. The view is of the east side from Northernhay to Upper Paul Street.

In 1865 work began on building the Royal Albert Memorial Museum on that site. It was later remembered that a row of houses had stood there, these are the buildings depicted in the sketch.[274] The Post Office building, situated alongside the museum, was also erected that year.

Corner of Queen Street and Paul Street, as depicted for 1860.
Redeveloped in the late nineteenth century.

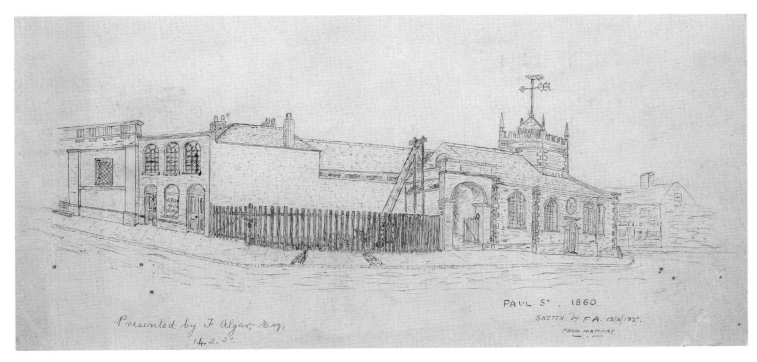

The corner site, Numbers 15 and 16 Queen Street, was redeveloped in 1851 and occupied in part or in whole by Carr & Quick, wine and spirit merchants, until 1961. Algar's drawing shows the firm was already there in 1860. H. Scott, depicted on the bottom of Goldsmith Street, was a butcher.[275] The building was demolished in the 1970s to create the Guildhall Shopping Centre.[276] The medieval church of St Paul had already been dismantled in 1936.[277]

99. First of four retrospective views by F. Algar of Queen Street in 1860, as drawn on 14 February 1927. It depicts Paul Street running from its corner with Queen Street on the left to Goldsmith Street on the right.

Queen Street between Paul Street and Northernhay Street, as depicted for 1860.
Redeveloped in 1878.

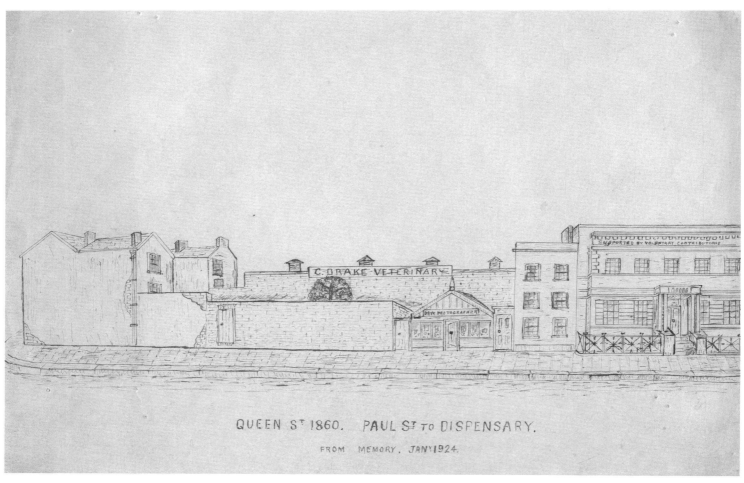

QUEEN S^T 1860.   PAUL S^T TO DISPENSARY.

FROM MEMORY. JAN^Y 1924.

100. Pen sketch by F. Algar, January 1924, of the corner of Queen Street with Paul Street in 1860. The view is from the Royal Albert Memorial Museum that was built five years later.

The Exeter Dispensary, shown to the far right, was opened on that site in 1841. The Museum Hotel is the building depicted to the left. It had been the private residence of Mr John Pidsley,[278] an attorney,[279] and was opened by 1878 but demolished in about 1926 to allow greater traffic flow into Paul Street. It was replaced by the Public Information Bureau which had been located several doors away. That building was later demolished for the Harlequin Shopping Centre in the 1980s.[280] E. Drake was a veterinary surgeon on Upper Paul Street.[281]

City Prison, as depicted for 1860.
Redeveloped in 1877.

The City Prison was demolished in 1876 after being made redundant by the building of the new county prison on New North Road in 1863. It was built from in November 1863 but the building remained empty for another thirteen years.[284] There were several competing schemes to erect a hotel and it was intended to use the

QUEEN ST 1860.   TOP OF NORTHERNHAY ST

CITY PRISON AND ALMSHOUSE   (END HOUSE OF A ROW)

OUTER WALL OF RED SANDSTONE.   DRAWN FROM MEMORY. FEB. 1924.

1818 to 1819 as a successor to Southgate prison: the first stone was laid on 4 June 1818 and the building was opened in late June 1819.[282] Prisoners were brought through Northernhay to Rougemont Castle. During the Assizes they were led in chains and shackles and watched by hundreds of spectators.[283] The site was sold

stone from the prison for the internal walls of the hotel.[285] The foundation stone of Rougemont Hotel was laid on 4 April 1877 and it opened on the 12th, and then once again officially on the 27th, of May 1879. Part of the prison was still standing when the hotel opened.[286] The hotel is currently under threat of demolition.

101. Retrospective pen sketch by F. Algar, dated February 1924, of 1860.

7. Bedford Street

Bedford Street was, for more than seven hundred years, until 1942, one of the most prestigious areas of the city: it had three important phases, first a house of the Black Friars (or Dominicans), then Bedford House and finally Bedford Circus.

102. Sketch of Bedford House, c.1700, showing two stories and multiple gables.

Bedford House, as depicted in about 1700.
Demolished in 1773 for civic improvements.

The Exeter townhouse of the Russell family, dukes of Bedford, acquired at the Reformation. It had been a Dominican friary from the early thirteenth century but the building was converted sometime after 1539. The townhouse harboured Queen Henrietta Maria during her pregnancy in the Civil War and it was there that Princess Henrietta Anne was born. The house was afterwards divided into tenements. In the 1770s plans were begun to erect Bedford Circus and in 1773 Bedford House was demolished.[287] The Circus was not completed until 1825.

These were regarded as the finest Georgian buildings in Exeter but were heavily damaged in the Luftwaffe bombing of Exeter in 1942 and shortly afterwards pulled down. The city's main Post Office building was erected on its site in the 1950s.

103. Photograph of Bedford Circus, c.1930. Undoubtedly this is one of the greatest losses to the city from the bombing in 1942.

Bedford Circus Theatre, drawn in 1823.
Destroyed by fire in 1885.

Two theatres stood in Bedford Street, both were destroyed by fire. The previous theatre had been renovated in 1819 and burnt down on 7 March 1820. The second theatre burnt to the ground in 1885. The theatres were situated near the Southernhay end of Bedford Street.

An earlier theatre was situated in Waterbeer Street, behind the Guildhall in what is now the Guildhall Shopping Centre. In 1787 it was replaced by the first of the two Bedford Street theatres. Bedford Street had become a fashionable Georgian development in the city partly because it formed a useful link to Southernhay and the fashionable district of St Leonards.

Not long after the theatre opened John and Charles Kemble and Sarah Siddons, some of the most popular actors of their time, appeared on stage. The theatre

104. Ink sketch by John Harris, 2 July 1823, of the Bedford Circus Theatre.

closed for a short while in 1823 owing to financial difficulties but it reopened and continued through to the end of the nineteenth century. Edmund Kean was another of the famous actors who frequently appeared in the city and many popular plays of the period were performed in Exeter as in other fashionable provincial centres. In the early nineteenth century the theatre benefited from Exeter being a garrison town and with its transport links to the increasingly popular coastal resorts of Sidmouth, Exmouth, Dawlish, Teignmouth and Torquay. Until the coming of the railway these watering places were the playgrounds of the more affluent visitor who included several days in Exeter as part of the long holiday period. A visit to the theatre was an expected activity for tourists wanting to engage with local gentry and middle-class society. The end of the French war in 1815 reopened the continent to English travel and it slowly diminished the number of these visitors to the South Devon coast and to Exeter. Increasingly the theatre relied upon local patronage. Upon the destruction of the second theatre building a new theatre was built at the top of Longbrook Street (see page 78).[288]

105. Unattributed watercolour of the theatre, c.1811, viewed from Southernhay West looking into Bedford Street. On the right is now Broadwalk House, built in 1974.

The Half Moon Inn, 22 High Street, as photographed in 1912.
Demolished in 1912.

At the west side of the entrance to Bedford Street from High Street stood the Half Moon Inn. It was one of the city's prominent inns and during the early nineteenth century was known for the tunes played by the coach guards on their bugles.[289] The building is remembered for Sullivan first playing the music of the Mikado to Gilbert.

It was demolished in 1912 but one of its ceilings has been preserved at the Royal Albert Memorial Museum. The building was shortly afterwards replaced by Lloyd's Bank. Deller's Café opened in December 1916 on the first floor and not long afterwards it claimed, with justification, that 'as a social centre, Deller's stands pre-eminent'. There were two other branches in 'Dellerland' at Paignton and Taunton.[290] The Exeter building was destroyed in 1942.[291]

106. Damaged photograph of the Half Moon Hotel, 1912. The advertisement was for 'a special novelty', the Royal Hungarian Midgets, who were appearing at the Hippodrome.

Deller's Café opened in one world war and ended in the next. In those twenty eight years the city of Exeter changed quite dramatically in the level of traffic in its streets: horse-cabs and electric trams were replaced by motor cars and although it was always a bustling city, particularly on market days, there was a marked increase in traffic. By 1930 the city comprised nearly 70,000 people and the boundaries had spread out into the growing suburbs. In 1914 the city was without a university: the University College of the South West of England was then located in the centre of the city in Gandy Street and moved to the Streatham Hall site only in 1922 but did not receive its university status until ten years after the war. The administration of the county was still run within Rougemont Castle. The High Street was filled with stores run and owned by local people but national chains were already a presence. In the years between the two world wars Exeter was bustling and Deller's Café became the fashionable place to go.

107. Undated view of the interior of Deller's Café, a great meeting place for Exeter before the Second World War.

8. Eastgate

One of the principal entrances to the city where the mayor welcomed visiting dignitaries and also held off attacking armies with the last threat from Parliament from 1645 to 1646. After the gate was destroyed in the late eighteenth century the area remained long identified as Eastgate.

The East Gate, as drawn in the late eighteenth century.
Demolished in 1784 to improve the flow of traffic.

A Roman way into the city, the gate was a medieval structure. In October 1784 the City Chamber agreed to pull down the East Gate and sell the building materials. Two months later they also agreed to pay the artist John

Hayman five guineas for his two drawings and to contribute an additional five guineas towards the costs of producing engravings of them.[292] The city's Receiver actually paid him fifteen pounds and fifteen shillings.[293] The building materials were sold and some of the medieval stone was used to construct Numbers 266-7 High Street, roughly where Boots is located today. Included in the fabric of this Georgian building was the statue of Henry VII that for nearly three centuries had looked out from the gate on the people of Exeter.[294]

108-109. Two drawings by Henry Oxenham copied by E. Shapter, 1844, probably from the aquatint of 1785, showing the internal and external sides of the East Gate. The statue of Henry VII can be seen in the central niche.

St John's Hospital, as depicted in 1824.
Demolished in 1880.

St John's Hospital, later known as St John's Hospital School, operated as a school from the 1530s and housed Exeter Free Grammar School until 1840. On 10 April 1880 a lecture was given on the history of the school, which was relocated and is now known as Exeter School, and four days later the Head Master gave a dinner for students and friends to bid a public farewell to the old building.[295] The building was demolished and the foundation stone of the Eastgate Coffee Tavern was laid by the Mayor on 2 August 1880.[296] He noted that the building would 'prove to be a blessing to hundreds of citizens, leading them into the paths of sobriety and good conduct'. It was also pointed out, by Robert Dymond, a local historian, that here 'was heard the measured tramp of Roman legions . . . the cries of rage and pain of the fugitives from the terrible encounter with the Danes on

110. Lithograph of St John's Hospital, 1824.

the heights of Pinhoe, the passage out . . . of the motley procession that attended the triumphant progress of William of Orange'. The building included red brick from Culm Davy and white brick dressing from Chudleigh. The architect was James Crocker, a local man. The foundations of one tower of the East Gate were exposed during building work as were a great number of bones. It was subsequently confirmed that a butcher shop had previously stood there.[297] The butcher may have been Mr Darke who had sold his building to the Improvement Commissioners in the 1830s.[298] The Eastgate Coffee Tavern was destroyed by the bombing of the city in 1942.

111. Undated photograph of the interior of the Arcade.

112. Drawing attributed to George Townsend of the south tower of the East Gate, 14 May 1880, which was exposed during building work. The 'subway' is most likely the entrance to the underground passages.

Old London Inn, 105 Paris Streets, as drawn in 1844 of how it looked in 1798.
Demolished in 1933 for traffic improvement.

The London Inn was known possibly as early as the fourteenth century and from 1794 as the Old London Inn. In the 1840s the inn lost its prominence as the railway replaced the coaches. It was later known as the Bude Haven Inn and subsequently shortened to the Bude Hotel. The names referred to its position on the London Road and later to the posting of carriages to north Cornwall. The building stood slightly to the east of the current corner of the two streets, in effect in what is now the middle of the junction. The hotel was one of the city's premier establishments but lost its position with the opening of the New London Inn (which was built directly across the street on the opposite side of the High Street). The Clarence and the Rougemont also eclipsed it. In 1833, when the city was trying to clean up the streets and alleys, complaints were made of pigs being kept in the inn's outhouses and of the state of the open sewers.[299] Five years later the inn was still large enough to include stabling for some 67 horses (with additional stabling in Sidwell Street).[300] It was a focus for the city for some celebrations: in the late nineteenth century it was a great public occasion to attend the tripe suppers annually served to celebrate the 5th of November.[301] There were unsuccessful attempts to sell the building at auction in 1927 and 1933[302] but it was successfully purchased by the city council in 1933 in order to improve the flow of traffic around what was a difficult corner. A city councillor paid for the last round of drinks in the hotel's lounge bar on 6 June 1933. It was said in 1933 that 'the Bude was born, as it will die, to the music of traffic'. The hotel was demolished that month[303] and a new building erected on part of the site in 1935 for L. H. Fearis Ltd, a Gloucester firm that already had a shop in Sidwell Street.[304] The new building subsequently housed the Co-operative and since the mid-1980s Next.

113. Drawing by Henry Oxenham with the date 1798, as copied by E. Shapter, 1844. On the left is noted 'The London Inn back door' and to the right 'House to let'.

New London Inn/Hotel, London Inn Square, as photographed in about 1920.
Demolished in 1936 to make way for a cinema.

The New London was situated at the opposite side of the street, at the north-east end of the High Street and opened in 1794. It was built on the site of the Oxford Inn. The first owner was John Land, previously at the Half Moon and the Old London Inn, and from 1868 by Robert Pople. In the early nineteenth century it was one of the city's principal hotels, attracting illustrious visitors such as the Duke of Wellington in 1819, but declined by the middle of the 1800s: in 1802 Robert Southey commented on its luxurious fittings, in 1866 one Londoner found it airy, spacious and old fashioned with the 'most antiquated waiters and servants', in 1874 a visitor from Walsall thought it 'to be as it was in the palmy days of the road' and in 1892 Beatrix Potter made a quick exit when she alighted from the bus 'with the wisdom of bitter experience . . . bowed out with profuse apologies'.[305] The inn was demolished in 1936 and some of the bricks were used to make foundations for other buildings. Some 300 tons of rubble were taken away.[306] It was replaced by the Savoy Cinema that was itself pulled down in 1987 in order to erect the retail building known as Roman Gate.

114. Undated photograph of the New London Inn.

115. Entry of Robert Louis Stevenson in the Visitors' Book of the hotel. He wrote 'I cannot go without recording my obligations to everyone in the house; if it is your fate to fall sick at an inn, pray heaven it may be the New London!'.

I cannot go without recording my obligations to everyone in the house: if it is your fate to fall sick at an inn, pray heaven it may be the new London! Robert Louis Stevenson

The Theatre Royal, as photographed in 1887.
Destroyed by fire in 1887.

The first theatre to be built outside the city walls whereas the two previous theatres were situated along Bedford Circus (see Illustrations 104-105). It was built in 1886 and destroyed, like its two predecessors, by fire the following year. A second building replaced it two years later that escaped the blitz only to be demolished in 1962. Shortly afterwards the office building known as Portland House was erected on the site.[307]

116. Photograph of the first Theatre Royal building at the top of Longbrook Street, 1887, immediately after the fire.

Conclusion

Over the last five centuries a variety of factors have caused topographical change in Exeter. Some buildings have been lost to fire, many more to war, either in the 1640s or 1940s, but the majority of change has occurred through a sense of improvement. This has taken many forms. In some instances commercial redevelopment has produced more modern buildings and there are other examples of change on aesthetic grounds such as much of the clearance of Cathedral Close. Improvement has also been about sanitation: in the 1920s and 1930s there was an admirable move to upgrade housing for the very poor. Many hundreds of people received adequate accommodation although many ancient buildings were destroyed. A hundred years before this, the terror of infectious disease made change all the more pressing and the city had individual buildings removed as well as entire streets re-planned to allow a better circulation of air and light.

However, the majority of individual changes have taken place because of a need to improve the flow of traffic. In 1933 one commentator noted that the Old London Inn 'will go the way of all very old things, and over the ground on which it stands traffic will spread itself like a river overflowing its bank. And that is always the story of progress'.[308] Others have also commented on increasing levels of traffic: in about 1901 one local man wrote 'Motor cars have come, and although we see little of them here, still, elsewhere they are used, and must eventually supercede horseflesh for drawing loads both of people and goods'.[309] As farsighted as he was, he would no doubt be surprised at the extent Exeter has changed in order to accommodate the successors to his horses and carts. It is hard to credit that until relatively recently traffic to and from Cornwall passed through the city and over Exe Bridge. Only later was Countess Wear Bridge built, with the notorious Exeter Bypass; the High Street had been the equivalent of the M5 for many hundreds of years. While it never had the volume of today, it does help in imagining the traffic that has historically passed through the city. Moreover, until the 1830s the streets had the added difficulty of being used as open markets. This makes it more understandable that local officials in the eighteenth century demolished the ancient gates, and in the nineteenth set back dozens of houses to widen the streets which were as little as twelve feet wide. At that time South and North Streets were similar in their width to Gandy Street today. Gridlock and traffic congestion were issues even in the eighteenth century. In the cause of traffic improvement many hundreds of Exeter's buildings have been demolished.

Slicing off the fronts of buildings was a less severe manner of change than that commonly used today. The fronts were lost but the back portions of the buildings remained. It would be easier to think that change in general was more incremental in the past. Mostly it was but there were distinct periods when there was large-scale change such as in the 1640s outside of the city walls, in the 1820s and 1830s with the street widening schemes of the 1820s and 1830s and the slum clearance of the 1920s. They may seem minor in respect to more modern changes but to contemporary Exeter, which was so much smaller, it must have seemed even more overwhelming.

The great changes of the last sixty years, when the centre of the city was effectively rebuilt, have brought about a dread of modern architecture. In addition, there should be a lesson in the high price of war. Exeter had been fortunate that this was the first war in three hundred years but only a fool would imagine it will be the last. How many of the buildings that the current generation takes for granted will one day be swept aside through bombing? In some ways it is easier to accept losses to the city when they are caused by war, it is less easily forgivable with self-inflicted loss. There remains a deep-seated resentment over the brutal way in which redevelopment took place immediately after the war. Throughout the city it is argued that whereas continental cities were rebuilt in traditional ways, Exeter destroyed much of what it had and embraced modern architecture. This could have been the making of the city but instead it was to a great extent built to a poor standard, lacking in imagination and style. This presents an opportunity and challenge to the current generation: to build, and also rebuild, in a manner that will successfully fill the footsteps of previous generations. It is a sad indictment of modern life if it is thought that it is no longer possible to add positively to the city's built heritage. It is inconceivable to think that the best of Exeter has passed, that we can contribute nothing of lasting value to leave to subsequent generations.

The key lies in ensuring that change is the same as progress; that a proposed building enhances the city and the demolition of existing buildings is publicly discussed with subsequent decisions based in part in considering the importance of local distinctiveness. There is still much of ancient Exeter to appreciate. The preservation and conservation of historic buildings often places a tremendous financial burden on subsequent generations: Regency Exeter would probably not have been able to maintain the ancient gates which today would be appreciated and no doubt be a boon to tourism. Bowhill House is an apt example of a building that has been admirably saved but has yet to find a sustainable use. Preservation and conservation need to be followed by a use that makes buildings relevant to modern needs and the lack of it for Bowhill threatens its survival. These issues will continue: in the near future one of the last open areas in the city, Rougemont Castle, will face its first change in use in nearly a thousand years. There are many other historic buildings that also have an uncertain future; for example the Rougemont Hotel is threatened by its owners with demolition. The disregard for the building's history of Victorian railway enthusiasm was signalled when it was renamed.

But there are tremendous opportunities: a Roman city lies beneath our feet and the ancient walls offer an untapped and remarkable pedestrian pathway around much of the city. There are many other buildings that can be developed to bring out the historic diversity of Exeter. For many hundreds of years there has been a pride in Exeter, in blending commercial influences with conservation and beauty, which has resulted in the city we have today. It is clear that for just as long there have been arguments in Exeter between those that want to save historic buildings and those that want to redevelop. All of our prized buildings have been erected on the sites of existing buildings as well as those that are the least loved. The challenge is to successfully balance the needs of a growing modern city with preserving its ancient heritage. It is now possible to make informed judgements on individual buildings because recent research in the city's unparalleled archives has produced more information than was ever known. Yet the pressures to develop are equally great, Exeter has an extraordinary growth rate and unlike many other English cities the ancient city is still the commercial centre.

The newest crossing over the river Exe, the pedestrian bridge currently being erected at Bonhay Road, is a symbol of what is achievable in modern design.

Inevitably it has already attracted criticism,
as any change does, but its vibrancy is encouraging for
the future. A city that does not develop is bound to
stagnate, as will a soulless concrete canyon. The
responsibility of the current generation is to continue
to seek improvement and progress, and not merely
change.

Illustration Sources

All illustrations are derived from the Westcountry Studies Library unless noted from the Devon & Exeter Institution (DEI), Devon Record Office (DRO), Exeter Cathedral Archives (ECA), Exeter City Museums and Art Gallery (RAMM), the Isca Collection or a private collection.

Introduction: page xv, *Exeter Flying Post*, 23 July 1904; page xv Braun and Hoghenbegh's map of 1618; page xvi Sutton Nicholl's map of 1723; page xvii J. Hayman's map of 1805; page xviii R. Brown's map of 1835; page xix Royal Albert Memorial Museum; page xx Royal Albert Memorial Museum, 77/1938/2; page xxii p&d06695; page xxii Royal Albert Memorial Museum; page xxiv H. Tapley Soper, *Devonshire Past and Present by pen and camera* (Derby and London, 1913); page xxviii p&d6530; page xxix p&d06873 and detail; page xxxi p&d7718.

The text: 1 p&d43753; 2 sc924; 3 H. Tapley Soper, Devonshire Past and Present by pen and camera; 4 p&d40066; 5 George Townsend and W. R. Best, *Sketches of Bygone Exeter* (Exeter, 1909); 6 p&d43612; 7 p&d42977; 8 p&d04739; 9 p&d06892; 10 p&d07360; 11 p&d07851; 12 RAMM, unlisted; 13 p&d4203; 14 RAMM, unlisted; 15 p&d4203; 16 p&d7689; 17 SC920; 18 George Townsend and W. R. Best, *Sketches of Bygone Exeter* (Exeter, 1909); 19 ee4679; 20 p&d4151; 21 p&d06982; 22 p&d05710; 23 p&d42372; 24 p&d43573-1; 25 RAMM, unlisted; 26 p&d04150; 27-35 Edward Pocknell, Collection of Devon and Exeter Photographs; 36 private collection, copy of photograph now held by the Royal Albert Memorial Museum; 37 p&d7250; 38 p&d06484; 39 p&d6982; 40 p&d07711 (the Isca Collection); 41 p&d42497; 42 p&d05619; 43 p&d40382; 44 p&d04980; 45 p&d05695; 46 p&d05696; 47 p&d04700; 48 p&d40384; 49 p&d05618; 50 p&d05617; 51 DEI, d1; 52 p&d43541; 53 p&d44144; 54 p&d43602; 55 p&d04206; 56 p&d7721; 57 George Townsend and W. R. Best, *Sketches of Bygone Exeter* (Exeter, 1909); 58 p&d06915; 59 p&d06917; 60 p&d06450; 61 p&d7277; 62 p&d06957; 63 p&d43573; 64 p&d41455; 65 eca7068/4; 66 John Rocque's map of Exeter, 1744; 67 DRO, Z19/2/4; 68 p&d05597; 69 George Townsend, *Sketches of Bygone Exeter* (Exeter, 1908); 70 p&d04978; 71 p&d41456; 72 DRO, Z19/2/4; 73 sc898; 74 p&d06911; 75 DEI, no reference; 76 p&d42663 (the Isca Collection); 77 p&d7306; 78 p&d07337; 79 p&d42951; 80 George Townsend and W. R. Best, *Sketches of Bygone Exeter* (Exeter, 1909); 81 James Crocker, *Sketches of Old Exeter* (London, 1886), plate xxii; 82-92 Edward Pocknell, Collection of Devon and Exeter Photographs; 93 RAMM, 77/1938/1; 94 p&d06985; 95 p&d44086; 96 p&d06944; 97 p&d43605; 98 p&d04164; 99 p&d07824; 100 p&d07823; 101 p&d07822 (the Isca Collection); 102 DRO, L1258/E/MP/5; 103 p&d42730; 104 DRO, Z19/2/4; 105 p&d06430; 106 p&d7164; 107 p&d43617; 108 p&d06914; 109 p&d06913; 110 *A new Guide to the city of Exeter and its environs* (Exeter, 1824); 111 p&d42116; 112 p&d06558; 113 p&d06874; 114 e/b/xo174; 115 p&d43509; 116 p&d07003.

Notes

1. *Exeter Flying Post*, 26 April 1882.
2. *Exeter Flying Post*, 5 July 1717 quoted by Robert Dymond, *Exeter and Neighbourhood under George the Third* (1879).
3. *An Archaeo-Historical Assessment of the Royal Clarence Hotel, Exeter* (Exeter Archaeology, report 98.03, January 1998), 2-3.
4. James Cossins, *Reminiscences of Exeter fifty years since* (Exeter, 1877), 38.
5. The Water Gate's history is questionable before the sixteenth century.
6. D. Portman, *Exeter Houses, 1400 - 1700* (Exeter, 1966), 55-6.
7. Portman, *Exeter Houses*, 36.
8. Portman, *Exeter Houses*, 57-9.
9. Hoskins, *Exeter*, 127.
10. Hoskins, *Exeter*, v.
11. George Oliver, *The History of the City of Exeter* (Exeter, 1884), 161, 165, 166, 175.
12. T. J. Northy, *Popular History of Exeter* (Exeter, 1886), 165.
13. E. A. Freeman, *Exeter* (London, 1890), 236, 219.
14. Harbottle Reed, 'Demolition of ancient buildings of Exeter during the last half century', (*Transactions of the Devonshire Association*, 58, 1931), 273.
15. W. G. Hoskins, *Two Thousand Years in Exeter* (Exeter, 1960), 133-4.
16. *Exeter Flying Post*, 5, 12, 26 January 1881. The paper noted 'within the last few days we have witnessed the taking down of the ten cells almshouses, another of the antiquated buildings on the Second Back Lane'.
17. Devon Record Office (afterwards DRO), 76/20/3, page 256.
18. DRO, 76/20/3, pages 306-7.
19. Dymond, *Exeter and Neighbourhood*, 1824.
20. *Prize essay on the history and antiquities of Exeter by our own board school boy* (Exeter, no date), 10.
21. For example, see *The Devonshire Chronicle and Exeter News*, 28 April 1833.
22. Todd Gray, *Travellers' Tales: Exeter* (Exeter, 2000), 42, 58, 148.
23. A. M. Shorto, *The Story of Exeter* (Exeter, 1911), 172.
24. Peter Thomas and Jacqueline Warren, *Aspects of Exeter* (Plymouth, 1980), 143.
25. Freeman, *Exeter*, 217.
26. Philip Chilwell De La Garde, 'High Street, Exeter' (*Transactions of the Exeter Diocesan Society*, VI, 1862), 254.
27. Gray, *Exeter: The Travellers' Tales*, 172.
28. DRO, 76/20/4, page 307.
29. De La Garde, 'High Street', 254.
30. Cossins, *Reminiscences*, 46.
31. W. G. Hoskins, *Devon* (Newton Abbot, London, 1954), 395.
32. DRO, 69/4.
33. Journal of William Nation, in private hands.
34. DRO, 76/20/4, page 311.
35. *Exeter Flying Post*, 26 May 1906 reciting a letter of 9 October 1854.
36. Another period could be in the first years of Norman Exeter when some 48 houses were demolished to clear the site for Rougemont Castle but the details for this are sketchy: Hoskins, *Exeter*, 26-8.
37. William Hurst lived there in the late 1570s: *St Nicholas' Priory, Exeter* (Exeter, 1999). 16.
38. Gray, *Exeter*, 14.
39. Mark Stoyle, 'Whole Streets Converted to Ashes': Property Destruction in Exeter during the English Civil War', *Southern History*, volume 16, 1994, 74-6.
40. Edward Ashworth, 'Account of the church of St Mary Major, Exeter, with reference to its being pulled down and replaced by a larger edifice' (*Transactions of the Exeter Diocesan Architectural Society*, volume ii, second series, 1872), 26.
41. Cossins, *Reminiscences*, 46.
42. DRO, D2/1866.
43. *Exeter Flying Post*, 5 November 1779.
44. Dymond, *Exeter and Neighbourhood*, 1772.
45. George Oliver, *The History of the City of Exeter* (Exeter, 1884), 173.
46. DRO, 76/20/3, page 386.
47. Robert Newton, *Eighteenth Century Exeter* (Exeter, 1984), 134-5.
48. DRO, 76/20/3, page 385.
49. *Exeter Flying Post*, 15 December 1831.
50. *Exeter Flying Post*, 6 September 1832.
51. Newton, *Eighteenth Century Exeter*, 162-6.
52. *The Western Times*, 18 May 1833.
53. Cossins, *Reminiscences*, 38.
54. DRO, 76/20/4, page 335.
55. Cossins, *Reminiscences*, 47.
56. Cossins, *Reminiscences*, 46.
57. *The Exeter Itinerary* (1828), 34.
58. DRO, 76/20/4, page 335.
59. *Exeter Flying Post*, 13 June 1833.
60. Thomas Shapter, *A history of the cholera in Exeter in 1832* (reprint Wakefield, 1971), 216.
61. *Exeter Flying Post*, 16 May 1833.
62. Northy, *Popular History of Exeter*, 158.
63. DRO, 76/20/3, page 309.
64. Shapter, *Cholera*, 16.
65. *Exeter Flying Post*, 26 May 1906, letter of Revd George Oliver of 1854.
66. DRO, 76/20/6, page 110.
67. *Besley's Exeter*, 1836.
68. *Express and Echo*, 12 September 1933, 5 July 1930, 13 October 1932, 30 June 1934, 3 November 1931.
69. *Express and Echo*, 24 June 1931.
70. John Allan, 'Raleigh Radford' (*Devon Archaeological Society Proceedings*, 56, 1998), 2-3.
71. Communication with John Allan.
72. Hoskins, *Exeter*, 132.
73. *Express and Echo*, 3 June 1911.
74. Cossins, *Reminiscences*, 48.
75. Jenkins, *Exeter*, 395.
76. DRO, Exeter St John/PV1.
77. DRO, petitions for faculties, Exeter St John/1.
78. Thomas and Warren, *Aspects of Exeter*, 80.

79. *Exeter's planning achievements* (Exeter, undated), 29.
80. For instance see Bridget Cherry and Nikolaus Pevsner, *The Buildings of England: Devon* (1989), 364.
81. Cherry and Pevsner, *Devon*, 114.
82. Eduardo Hoyos-Saavedra, *Discovering Exeter: Twentieth Century Architecture* (Exeter Civic Society, 2001).
83. Peter Thomas, *Exeter Yesterday and Today* (Stroud, 2000), 44-5.
84. A. Jenkins, *Civil and Ecclesiastical History of the City of Exeter* (Exeter, 1806), 429.
85. DRO, 3992/H5/6.
86. Report of the Committee of Management, 1868.
87. DRO, 3992/H5/6/page 138.
88. Cossins, *Reminiscences*, 65.
89. DRO, 3992/H5/6/page 508.
90. Hazel Harvey, *Discovering Exeter 6 West of the River* (Exeter Civic Society, 1989) 13.
91. C. G. Henderson, 'The city of Exeter from AD 50 to the early nineteenth century', in Roger Kain and William Ravenhill, *Historical Atlas of South-West England*, (Exeter, 1999), 489.
92. *Express and Echo*, 1 July 1911.
93. Maurice Exwood and H. L. Lehmann (eds), *William Schellinks' Travels in England, 1661-1663* (Camden Society Fifth Series, 1, 1993), 111.
94. Oliver, *History*, 169-73.
95. Gray, *Exeter*, 45.
96. Hoskins, *Exeter*, 47.
97. Beatrix Cresswell, *Rambles in Old Exeter* (Exeter, 1927), 114.
98. George Townsend and W. R. Best, *Sketches of Bygone Exeter* (Exeter, 1909).
99. Lieut. Col. Harding, 'A paper on the churches and chantry of the ancient Exe bridge', *Transactions of the Exeter Diocesan Architectural Society*, Vol. 3, 1849, page 170.
100. DRO, ECA/petitions/5/43.
101. H. Tolson, *Exeter and its bridges* (Exeter, c.1901), 10.
102. The date was given by Samuel Poole in his diary: DRO, 5183/Z1.
103. Oliver, *History*, 169.
104. DRO, ECA/Receiver's Account Book 122.
105. DRO, ECA/Receiver's Account Book 124.
106. Northy, *Popular History of Exeter*, 167.
107. Oliver, *History*, 172.
108. *Express & Echo*, 27 August 1938.
109. Oliver, *History*, 161.
110. Cossins, *Reminiscences*, 58.
111. Reed, 'Demolition', 281.
112. H. Tolson, *Exeter and its bridges*, 11-12.
113. DRO, ECA/Chamber Minute Book 25, meetings 27 November 1770, 29 January 1771, 29 October 1771, 16 November 1771.
114. *Express and Echo*, 1 July 1911.
115. Jenkins, *Exeter*, 212.
116. *The Western Times*, July 1899.
117. *The Post Office Directory of Exeter and Suburbs for 1897-8* (Exeter, 1898).
118. Mary Ravenhill and Margery Rowe (eds), *Devon Maps and Mapmakers* (Devon & Cornwall Record Society), forthcoming.
119. Jeffery was listed in *The Exeter Itinerary* as an artist resident in Paris Street in 1835. Several of his pictures are held by the Royal Albert Memorial Museum.
120. He was born in about 1806 and died in 1874, aged 68:

121. Todd Gray, *Exeter Engraved: volume one* (Exeter, 2001), 140.
122. *Exeter Flying Post,* 25 January, 2 August 1882.
123. It was presumably named after the former building at Number 185 which it replaced: *Exeter Flying Post,* 25 January 1882.
124. Reed, 'Demolition', 280.
125. *Exeter Itinerary and General Directory* (1828).
126. *Besley's Exeter*, 1861-81.
127. *Besley's Illustrated Handbook of Exeter* (Exeter, 1890), 108.
128. Robert Dymond, *Exeter and Neighbourhood*, 1769.
129. Cossins, *Reminiscences*, 46.
130. DRO, 74/3/321.
131. Northy, *Popular History of Exeter*, 165-6.
132. DRO, ECA/plan R16.
133. *Woolmer's Exeter and Plymouth Gazette*, 10 February 1821.
134. Exeter Dean and Chapter Archives, CC38/75793. I am grateful to Tony Collings for this reference.
135. Exeter Dean and Chapter Archives, CC38/75793.
136. DRO, 74/3/336. I am grateful to Tony Collings for this reference.
137. Jenkins, *Exeter*, 361-2.
138. Thomas George Norris, 'A paper on the statue of S. Peter, North Street, Exeter', *Transactions of the Exeter Diocesan Architectural Society* (volume one, second series, 1867), 159-62. R. W. Parker has given the date of the building as either late fifteenth or early sixteenth century: R. W. Parker, *Archaeological Recording at No. 2 Broadgate, Exeter*, Exeter Archaeology Report No. 97.73, October 1997, page 17.
139. DRO, 74/3/321.
140. Cossins, *Reminiscences*, 13.
141. Exeter Dean & Chapter Archives, CC38/75793.
142. The firm had been there from at least 1816: *The Exeter Pocket Journal*, 1816.
143. Reed, 'Demolition', 277.
144. Cresswell, *Rambles*, 17.
145. Cossins, *Reminiscences*, 46.
146. Norris, 'Statue', 160.
147. *Woolmer's Exeter and Plymouth Gazette*, 10 & 17 February 1821.
148. Norris, 'Statue', 160-1.
149. Jenkins, *Exeter*, 360-1.
150. *Exeter and Plymouth Gazette*, 24 November 1881; *Western Morning News*, 13 October 1906.
151. *West of England Pocket Book*, 1847.
152. *The Exeter Itinerary*, 1835.
153. James Crocker, *Sketches of Old Exeter* (London, 1886), plate vii.
154. G. C. Dunning, 'The horse and knight roof finial, with a discussion of knight and roof finials in England and on the continent'(*Bedfordshire Archaeology*, 9, 1974), 117.
155. Thomas and Warren, *Aspects of Exeter*, 92-3.
156. Gray, *Exeter: The Travellers' Tales*, 172.
157. The date was given by William Nation in his journal: the diary of William Nation in private hands.
158. DRO, Chanter 1477.
159. James Cossins, *Reminiscences*, 46.
160. Discussions were held by the Commissioners to take down houses in South Street in 1829: Dymond, *Exeter and Neighbourhood*, 1829.
161. DRO, Chanter 1477.

Devon & Exeter Institution Library, file cards on Devon artists by Sam Smiles.

162. The Commissioners were still discussing repairs on 8 May and its replacement on the 15th of that month. They had discussed pulling it down in May 1833: *Exeter Flying Post*, 8, 15 May 1834, 16 May 1833.

163. It may have been 20th November: *Vincent's Guide to Exeter* (Exeter, 1884), vii.

164. Northy, *Popular History of Exeter*, 157.

165. Cossins, *Reminiscences*, 57.

166. A correspondent to *The Gentleman's Magazine* suggested it was built in the reign of Henry VII: *The Gentleman's Magazine*, Vol IX, May 1838, page 484-6.

167. H. Lloyd Parry and Harold Brakspear, with revisions by Joyce Youings, *St. Nicholas' Priory Exeter* (Exeter, 1960), 18; Bernard W. Hely, *Historical Notes on English Catholic Missions* (1907), 171.

168. Jenkins, *Exeter*, 383.

169. *Exeter Flying Post*, 9 March 1815, 12 June 1817.

170. DRO, 5200 add 5c/156/3; D2/1598(i).

171. DRO, ECA/Exeter valuation list 1838.

172. *Besley's Exeter 1878*.

173. Paper read in 1881, *Transactions of the Exeter Diocesan Architectural Society*, second series, volume iv, 328-9.

174. Westcountry Studies Library, folder on King John's Tavern, note regarding Dymond's Mss.

175. *Besley's Exeter* (Exeter, 1924).

176. Robert Dymond, 'The Old Inns and Taverns of Exeter', *Transactions of the Devonshire Association*, 1880.

177. Jenkins, *Exeter*, 382.

178. DRO, D2/1595(i).

179. 'St George's Church, South Street, Exeter', *Devon & Cornwall Notes & Queries*, vol. 2, 1902, page 6.

180. *Besley's Exeter*, 1842.

181. There is also a tradition that it was the town house of the Abbots of Tavistock. Both theories have slender evidence.

182. Jenkins, Exeter, 370.

183. Cossins, *Reminiscences*, 58.

184. The diary of William Nation, March 1805: private hands.

185. *The Exeter Journal*, 1845.

186. *Besley's Exeter 1878*.

187. *Besley's Exeter 1881*. 188. *The Western Antiquary*, February 1883.

189. Hugh Mellor, *Exeter Architecture* (Chichester, 1989), 83.

190. *Besley's Exeter*, 1853.

191. Ethel Lega-Weekes, *Some Studies in the Topography of the Cathedral Close, Exeter* (Exeter, 1915), 114, manuscript notes in the author's copy held at the Westcountry Studies Library.

192. I am grateful to Tony Collings for this information.

193. *The Exeter Itinerary* (Exeter, 1828), 41.

194. DRO, D7/550/1-6.

195. Census, 1851, Holy Trinity parish.

196. Census, 1871, Holy Trinity parish.

197. Besley's Exeter Journal, 1883.

198. I am grateful to John Allan for this information.

199. Cossins, *Reminiscences*, 44-5.

200. Edmund Granger noted it in his diary: DRO, 69/4, page 37.

201. DRO, 76/20/3, page 169.

202. Oliver, *History*, 166.

203. DRO, 76/20/3, page 169.

204. Jenkins, *Exeter*, 371.

205. DRO, 1718Aadd/PW3; Cossins, *Reminiscences*, 49.

206. DRO, ECA, Receiver's Account Book 200-202.

207. DRO, ECA/Exeter valuation list 1838.

208. Cossins, *Reminiscences*, 47-8.

209. Jenkins, *Exeter*, 383.

210. DRO, 76/20/5, page 109; George Oliver wrote that the foundation stone was laid on the 4th day of April and that it opened on the 9th day of December: Oliver, *History*, 173-4.

211. DRO, 76/20/3, page 168.

212. DRO, 69/4, page 99.

213. Portman, *Exeter Houses*, 5.

214. Oliver, *History*, 173.

215. Lega Weekes, *The Close*, 127-8.

216. Information supplied by Richard Parker.

217. Exeter Cathedral Archives, D&C, 7068/4.

218. Exeter Cathedral Archives, 7068/4.

219. Exeter Cathedral Archives, 3578, page 293.

220. Exeter Cathedral Archives, 7068/4. Other items included a red deal floor and an 'old brick' floor.

221. *Woolmer's Exeter and Plymouth Gazette*, 17 February 1821.

222. Exeter Cathedral Archives, 3578.

223. Edward Ashworth, 'Account of the church of St Mary Major, Exeter, with reference to its being pulled down and replaced by a larger edifice', *Transactions of the Exeter Diocesan Architectural Society*, volume ii, second series, 1872, 24-8.

224. Thomas Granger remembered it moving to Gandy Lane on 13 May 1809 and moving to Bedford Lane on 18 November 1812: DRO, 69/4.

225. *The Western Luminary*, 20 September 1853.

226. Cossins, *Reminiscences*, 42.

227. R. W. Parker, *Archaeo-Historical Assessment of Exeter Cathedral Cloisters* (Exeter Archaeology, report 97.42, June 1997), 24-5.

228. Exeter Cathedral Archives, 3776/1/4, pages 56-7.

229. Parker, *Archaeo-Historical Assessment of Exeter Cathedral Cloisters*, 25-6.

230. Michael Fodor, *Discovering Exeter 8/Gates of the Close* (Exeter, 1996), 32.

231. Exeter Cathedral Archives, 3577, page 528. He took the place of the Porter of the Close.

232. Exeter Cathedral Archives, 3579, pages 4, 149-50.

233. Angela Doughty, 'The Gates of the Close', *Friends of Exeter Cathedral 66th Annual Report* (1992), 19-20.

234. *Woolmer's Exeter and Plymouth Gazette*, 20 March 1825.

235. DRO, 69/4, pages 57-8.

236. Cossins, *Reminiscences*, 46.

237. *Exeter Flying Post*, 30 December 1824.

238. DRO, 76/20/3, page 306-7.

239. Doughty, 'Gates', 19-20.

240. DRO, 76/20/4, 311.

241. Thomas and Warren, *Aspects of Exeter*, 137.

242. Exeter Cathedral Archives, D&C 6008/3/7. I am grateful to Tony Collings for this information.

243. Andrew Brice, *The Mobiad* (Exeter, 1770), 169.

244. *Express & Echo*, 8 May 1974, letter of Professor John Caldwell.

245. Crocker, *Exeter*, plate 22.

246. *Exeter Itinerary and General Directory*, 1828

247. Oliver, *Exeter*, 160.

248. DRO, 69/4, page 44.

249. *Exeter Flying Post*, 10 November 1880.

250. *Exeter Flying Post*, 3 November 1880.

251. *Protestant Mercury*, 10 January 1715.

252. DRO, ECA/Exeter valuation list 1838.

253. DRO, 76/20/5, page 223.

254. Cossins, *Reminiscences*, 38; *The Exeter Journal*, 1836.

255. DRO, 76/20/5, pages 223, 295.
256. Census of 1851, All Hallows Goldsmith parish.
257. *West of England Pocket Book*, 1847, page 240.
258. Census of 1851, All Hallows Goldsmith parish.
259. Thomas, *Exeter Yesterday and Today*, 62.
260. Sidney Stoyle was there until 1878, followed by J. Herbert Maggs until 1882, then Cross & Johnson until 1891, William Lyon & Company until 1895 and Wheaton until 1928: *Besley's Exeter Journals*, 1878-1929.
261. Thomas and Warren, *Aspects of Exeter*, 165.
262. Thomas, *Exeter Yesterday and Today*, 62.
263. Census of 1851, All Hallows Goldsmith parish.
264. *Besley's Exeter Journals*, 1881-1933.
265. Census of 1851, All Hallows Goldsmith parish.
266. Thomas and Warren, *Aspects of Exeter*, 213-214.
267. *Besley's Exeter*, 1828, 1842.
268. Census of 1851, All Hallows Goldsmith parish.
269. *Besley's Exeter Journals*, 1852-1951.
270. H. Lloyd Parry, *Exeter Guildhall* (Exeter, 1936), 106-7.
271. *Besley's Exeter Journals*.
272. Cossins, *Reminiscences*, 17.
273. *Exeter Flying Post*, 1 July 1911; Westcountry Studies Library, Exeter Newspaper Cuttings 1909-1912.
274. Cossins, *Reminiscences*, 38.
275. *Besley's Exeter*, 1863.
276. Thomas, *Exeter Yesterday and Today*, 67.
277. Thomas, *Exeter Yesterday and Today*, 81.
278. Cossins, *Reminiscences*, 39.
279. *The Exeter Itinerary*, 1828, 1834.
280. Thomas, *Exeter Yesterday and Today*, 64, 83.
281. *Besley's Exeter*, 1863.
282. DRO, 69/4.
283. Cossins, *Reminiscences*, 59.
284. W. J. Forsythe, *A system of discipline, Exeter borough prison, 1819-1863* (Exeter, 1983), 92.
285. *Exeter Flying Post*, 26 January 1876.
286. *Devon & Exeter Gazette*, 31 January 1930; *Exeter Flying Post*, 12 & 27 May 1879.
287. D. Portman, *Exeter Houses, 1400 - 1700* (Exeter, 1966), 37.
288. DRO, 69/4, page 38; Newton, *Eighteenth Century Exeter*, 70, 130.
289. Cossins, *Reminiscences*, 53.
290. *About Dellerland: Exeter, Paignton and Taunton* (Exeter, no date), 21.
291. Hoskins, *Exeter*, 127-8.
292. DRO, ECA/Chamber Act Book 16, 12 October and 17 December 1784.
293. DRO, ECA/Receiver's Account Book 144.
294. Thomas and Warren, *Aspects of Exeter*, 215.
295. *Exeter Flying Post*, 14 April 1880 and 12 January 1881.
296. Northy, *Popular History of Exeter*, 169.
297. *The Western Times*, 3 August 1880.
298. *Exeter Flying Post*, 20 June 1833.
299. *Exeter Flying Post*, 13 June 1833.
300. DRO, ECA/Exeter valuation list 1838.
301. *Exeter Flying Post*, 26 January 1881, page 7.
302. *Express & Echo*, 2 May 1927, 9 March 1933.
303. *Express & Echo*, 7 June 1933, 20 April 1933.
304. *Express & Echo*, 14 March 1935.
305. Gray, *Travellers' Tales*, 101, 139, 141, 158.
306. *Express & Echo*, 10 February 1936.
307. Dick Passmore, *The Story of the Theatre Royal Exeter* (Exeter, 2002), 8-22, 106, 110-111.
308. *Express & Echo*, 20 April 1933.
309. H. Tolson, *Exeter and its bridges* (Exeter, c.1901), 10.